100
GREATS

ST HELENS
RLFC

STADIA

100
GREATS

ST HELENS
RLFC

ALEX SERVICE SAINTS HERITAGE SOCIETY

Saints Heritage Society

The main aim of the Society is to collect, exhibit and interpret documents, images and artefacts relating to the history of the St Helens Rugby League Club. By doing this we are aiming to be a premier research institution, expand audiences for the history of rugby league and help to create a permanent Heritage Centre within any new stadium development by the club. Our website (www.saints.org.uk) was opened on 26 November 2003 by Saints' 'Great' Geoff Pimblett and this 'virtual heritage centre' has become one of the most innovative and informative sites in British sport. We deal with enquiries from all over the world about matters relating to the history of St Helens RLFC and have established strong links with the parent club and Past Players Association. Achievements of past players have been celebrated by Milestones Awards and the Society continues actively to promote the rich heritage and historical tapestry of the St Helens Club.

First published 2006

STADIA is an imprint of
Tempus Publishing Limited
The Mill, Brimscombe Port,
Stroud, Gloucestershire, GL5 2QG
www.tempus-publishing.com

© Alex Service, 2006

British Library Cataloguing in Publication Data.
A catalogue record for this book is available from the British Library.

ISBN 0 7524 4079 9

Typesetting and origination by Tempus Publishing Limited.
Printed in Great Britain.

Foreword

Over the years I have played with and coached some of the greatest players ever seen at St Helens Rugby League Club. You have to earn the tag, and it can be for a number of reasons. You do assume these people are great rugby players in their own right, but they should have the ability to go out and do something special to win a match, in the first or the seventy-ninth minute! Saints have always had players like this, with tremendous talent and flair. My first coach, the great Jim Sullivan, made sure we could all pass, run and tackle to a very high standard indeed. He drummed it into us that winning was the ultimate aim, but we were never coached to play negative football – that was never the way at Knowsley Road! There are also those who assume the mantle of greatness through their sheer application, enthusiasm and dedication, who would get stuck in when we were getting laid on away from home, at places like Workington and Featherstone!

It was a real privilege to play in the same side as so many great footballers at Saints. Glyn Moses was a brilliant full-back and it was virtually unheard of for anyone to run round or through him. Austin Rhodes could play with distinction anywhere from numbers one to six! Tom van Vollenhoven in his prime was probably the best winger you will ever see! Duggie Greenall was his first centre, with great hands and was a really rugged defender. What about Tommy Bishop, who joined us from Barrow in 1966 and became a world-class No.7? Then there was Len Killeen – a fantastic kicker with a brilliant pair of hands. Who could ever forget the sheer courage of Alan Prescott, who led us to victory in the Second Test at Brisbane with a broken arm? Names like Cliff Watson and Vince Karalius put the fear of God into the opposition and the likes of Dick Huddart, who would be absolutely unstoppable in today's game. He had magnificent hands and the ability to transfer the ball from one hand to the other at speed so that he could operate that jack-hammer hand-off!

I have also worked with some magnificent players when I coached at St Helens, like Chris Arkwright, a big, strong lad who could play in a number of positions, particularly stand-off and loose forward. Shane Cooper had incredible hands and an uncanny ability to read a game. Roy Haggerty – what a player he was! Ask anyone who ever played with him if you don't believe me! Paul Loughlin, Barrie Ledger, Neil Holding, Phil Veivers… the list goes on. I'm sure like me you will enjoy the contents of this book and recall the deeds of the greatest players who have worn the famous red and white jersey over the years. Picking a best-ever XIII is a difficult task indeed!

Alex Murphy OBE
St Helens
December 2005

Introduction

This collection represents a real cross-section of players who have made, in their own particular way, a significant contribution to the achievements of the St Helens Rugby League Club since 1895. The top twenty players here are on a par with anyone ever seen in this great game of ours and most come from the post Second World War era, with sixteen playing in the Super League competition from 1996.

Most players featured here have played 200 matches, although there are many other qualities and achievements that make a 'great', such as the ability to turn a game with a touch of brilliance. There are prolific try-scorers, like Tom van Vollenhoven; fantastic goal kickers like Kel Coslett and the best player in a particular position, such as Alex Murphy – a scrum-half in a million! What about overseas stars like the Super League sensation of 2005, Jamie Lyon? There are also players who gave two hundred percent on the field and became cult figures with the fans, like Roy Haggerty. Many gained further fame in the international arena, like the legendary loose forward Vince Karalius – the 'Wild Bull of the Pampas'.

It must not be forgotten that there are many players not included here who would be automatic first choices for other clubs in a similar publication. This book will undoubtedly get people talking about their favourite players and, above all, the team that has meant so much to them over the years – the mighty Saints!

Acknowledgements

Although this book highlights the achievements of great individuals, its compilation has been the result of great team-work.

The photographs in this book have been provided by Bernard Platt, Brian Peers, John Riding, Robert Gate, Curtis Johnstone and publications such as *The Rugby Leaguer*, *St Helens Reporter* and *St Helens Star*.

Bill Bates, Denis Whittle, Dave Dooley and Paul Cunliffe, my fellow members of the Saints' Heritage Society, have played major roles. I would also like to thank members of the St Helens Past Players Association, especially Secretary Geoff Pimblett, Duggie Greenall and 'Senior pro' Jimmy Goodier for their help and advice. From the Saints' Original Supporters Club, John Powell, Gerry Moore and Brian Potter have given me the benefit of their wide knowledge of Saintly matters, although they will always agree to disagree about the choice of players in this book!

Special thanks to one of our all-time greats, Alex Murphy OBE, for providing such an appropriate foreword. Finally, on behalf of the Saints' Heritage Society, I would like to dedicate this book to everyone who has represented our team – and our town – in the greatest game of all!

Alex Service
St Helens
December 2005

100 St Helens Greats

Darren Albert
Chris Arkwright
Jack Arkwright
Len Aston
Bob Atkin
Frank Barrow
Tom Barton
Billy Benyon
Tommy Bishop
Jack Bradbury
William Briers
Frank Carlton
Eric Chisnall
Bill Clarey
Gary Connolly
Shane Cooper
Kel Coslett
Charlie Crooks
Eddie Cunningham
Keiron Cunningham
Bob Dagnall
Bob Doherty
Bernard Dwyer
Alf Ellaby
Les Fairclough
David Fairleigh
Albert Fildes
Jim Flanagan
Paul Forber
Tom Foulkes
Ray French
Alf Frodsham
Peter Glynn
Peter Gorley

Bobbie Goulding
Duggie Greenall
Walter Groves
Roy Haggerty
Ben Halfpenny
Roy Hardgrave
Jeff Heaton
Neil Holding
Sean Hoppe
Lou Houghton
Dick Huddart
Alan Hunte
Kevin Iro
Mel James
Les Jones
Chris Joynt
Tony Karalius
Vince Karalius
Len Killeen
Barrie Ledger
Frank Lee
George Lewis
Graham Liptrot
Stewart Llewellyn
Sean Long
Paul Loughlin
Jamie Lyon
George Mann
John Mantle
Tommy Martyn
Roy Mathias
Stan McCormick
Mal Meninga
Bill Mercer

Glyn Moses
Alex Murphy
Frank Myler
Paul Newlove
George Nicholls
Sonny Nickle
George Parsons
Apollo Perelini
Geoff Pimblett
Harry Pinner
Andrew Platt
Alan Prescott
James Prescott
Austin Rhodes
Tea Ropati
Paul Sculthorpe
Nat Silcock
Wilf Smith
Jimmy Stott
Anthony Sullivan
Mick Sullivan
Abe Terry
Hubert Turtill
Tom van Vollenhoven
Phil Veivers
John Walsh
Kevin Ward
John Warlow
Cliff Watson
Paul Wellens
William Whiteley
Frank Wilson

The twenty who appear here in italics occupy two pages instead of the usual one.

Statistical note:

The career summary for each player included in this volume relates to appearances and scores for St Helens only.
All statistics are up to the end of the 2005 Super League season.
Representative honours include those won by the player when with the St Helens club.
All official competitive fixtures played by the club, from 1895-2005, are included in players' career totals
Substitute appearances, introduced in 1964, are included.
Career details are from the advent of the Northern Rugby Football Union in 1895.

Darren Albert

Winger 2002-2005

Previous club: Newcastle Knights (Australia)

St Helens debut: 10 February 2002 v. Oldham

Final St Helens appearance: 11 September 2005 v. Wigan Warriors

Appearances: 124

Tries: 88

Goals: 0

Points: 352

Transferred to: Cronulla Sharks (Australia)

Representative honours: None

Born in Auburn, Australia on 28 February 1976, Darren Albert has won Grand Finals in both hemispheres. A NSW and Country of Origin representative, he was a member of the 1997 Newcastle Knights team that defeated Manly, with Albert himself scoring the winning try in the last seconds of the match. He has also achieved Grand Final glory with St Helens (2002), together with a Challenge Cup winner's medal in 2004. The secret of Albert's success was pace. He was officially the 'fastest man' in Super League and used this as a basis for scoring tries from anywhere on the field.

Although tending to be a straight runner, relying on his speed along the touchline, rather than sidestep or swerve, Darren had excellent hands, exemplified by his diving catch from a Sean Long chip to score a brilliant try in the wet at Widnes Vikings in 2005. Seemingly unflappable, Darren was an extremely durable footballer, rarely missing a match in his four seasons at Knowsley Road and became a real crowd favourite. Another vital ingredient of his success was his defensive ability. His tackling technique was superb and he could bring down the likes of Bradford's 'Man Mountain' Lesley Vainikolo with seemingly little difficulty. His speed enabled him to cover any opposition breaks in other areas of the field. One cover tackle, against London's Andrew King, at Brentford in 2003 simply defied logic, just as he looked odds on to score.

Darren was versatile and could play with equal effectiveness in the centres, or at full-back, where he was able to make the most of his ability in 'broken field' situations. He won a Grand Final ring in his first season as St Helens beat Bradford Bulls 19-18 in a tense battle at Old Trafford. Darren led the scorers with 25 touchdowns from 37 appearances; a feat he was able to do once more in 2003, although he was joint leading scorer with fellow Australian Darren Smith, on 19 from 28 starts. Albert was unlucky not to get on the scoresheet at the Millennium Stadium during the Saints' 32-16 defeat of rivals Wigan in the 2004 Challenge Cup final, but yet again, he made the most appearances during the season, scoring 16 tries, four behind Jason Hooper.

The arrival of centre Jamie Lyon in 2005 proved to be sensational for Darren. The pair seemed to gel immediately and became the most potent attacking partnership in the British game, contributing 52 tries between them in League and Cup. It was such a pity that Albert shattered his cheekbone late in the campaign against Wigan – one of a series of injuries that wrecked the Saints' Grand Final hopes. At the end of the season, Darren moved to Cronulla to finish off his career back home in the NRL. His try-scoring feats for St Helens, in particular, are the stuff of legend.

Chris Arkwright
Centre, stand-off, loose forward 1978-1990

Previous club: St Helens Colts

St Helens debut: 22 October 1978 v. Warrington

Final St Helens appearance: 22 April 1990 v. Bradford Northern

Appearances: 249 + 24 subs

Tries: 90

Goals: 0

Points: 322

Transferred to: Runcorn Highfield

Representative honours: Lancashire, England, Great Britain

Signed from the St Helens Colts team on 6 October 1978 and making his first team debut just two weeks later, Chris Arkwright had an immaculate family pedigree, with both his father and grandfather playing for the club. The Saints were in a transitional phase at the time and Chris was one of a number of local lads, like Barrie Ledger, Steve Peters and Neil Holding, who were to provide the backbone of the squad over the next few years.

Chris scored his first try for the club in the match against Leigh on 3 November 1978 and never looked back. He was a powerfully built runner, with a neat sidestep and was a great opportunist, leading the Saints' try-scorers on two consecutive occasions in the early 1980s. An uncompromising character, he also began to show his versatility, operating equally effectively at centre, stand-off or loose forward. Arkwright's form was such that he was selected for the 1984 Australian tour squad, yet he was sensationally withdrawn by the League's doctor seven days later as a result of knee trouble and was replaced by Oldham's Terry Flanagan.

The signing of Australians Mal Meninga and Phil Veivers proved to be the springboard for success in the 1984/85 campaign and this brought out the best in Chris Arkwright, including a stunning hat-trick in the 48-16 defeat of Leeds in a League match at Knowsley Road on 9 December 1984. He was also a member of the side which beat Wigan in the Lancashire Cup final at Central Park and followed this with a brilliant performance at stand off in the Premiership final against Hull KR at Elland Road, when the Saints produced some sparkling football in a memorable 36-16 success.

Chris won a place in the Great Britain squad for the home series against the Kiwis in 1985, captained by his teammate Harry Pinner. Ironically, it was Arkwright who replaced Pinner as Saints' captain and the side produced some superb open rugby in the 1986/87 season. Operating at loose forward, he ran in for 20 tries and led the side against Halifax at Wembley in the Challenge Cup final. Success would have been the highlight of Arkwright's club career, yet Halifax just pipped a somewhat nervous Saints outfit by 19-18.

Unfortunately, injury started to blight his career, especially after the 1987/88 season and he was to wear the famous red vee on just thirteen occasions afterwards. Many rugby league players would have been content to have gained two Great Britain caps, one England jersey and played for their county on four occasions – yet even this impressive list of honours fails to recognise just how good a footballer Chris Arkwright really was.

Jack Arkwright

Second-row forward 1928-1934

Previous club: Sutton Commercial

St Helens debut: 8 December 1928 v. Oldham

Final St Helens appearance: 10 September 1934 v. Rochdale Hornets

Appearances: 174

Tries: 39

Goals: 21

Points: 159

Transferred to: Warrington

Representative honours: Lancashire, England

Opinion was very often divided as to the merits of 'Big' Jack Arkwright, but to many, he was one of the greatest rugby league forwards in the 1930s. 'He was a grand scrummager,' wrote the noted St Helens journalist Tom Reynolds. 'He could handle like a threequarter. He could kick goals. He could score tries. In Australia he was regarded as one of the most efficient forwards who had ever come out with a visiting side.' Born in Rolling Mill Lane, Sutton in 1902, Jack was a late developer in rugby league terms, switching from soccer in his late twenties to play with his local Sutton Commercial club. Batley and Warrington showed interest, but after playing several matches in the 'A' team at Knowsley Road, he became a Saint for a £50 fee in December 1928.

A huge man, at 6ft 3ins and fifteen stone, with a fifteen-inch hand span, Arkie first made a name for himself as an emergency kicker in the Saints-Recs Challenge Cup tie at Knowsley Road in 1930, where his three goals helped the home side to a 9-7 victory in the mud. Jack went on to play in all the succeeding rounds before being left out of the side which eventually lost to Widnes 10-3 at Wembley. Although bitterly disappointed, he went on to help the Saints to their first-ever Championship final success, against Huddersfield in 1932. Supremely fit and capable of 100 yards in eleven seconds, Jack also scored one of the quickest tries on record, against Leigh, when he caught the ball straight from the kick-off and powered his way under the posts.

By 1932/33, financial pressures saw many top names depart from Knowsley Road. The Saints' committee decided to try and build a team round Arkwright's giant frame, but it was not to be. He was transferred to Warrington for a world-record £800 fee at the start of the 1934/35 season and won two Championship runners-up medals and a Challenge Cup runners-up medal in 1936.

Jack made his debut for Lancashire in a 3-9 reversal against Cumbria at Barrow on 15 October 1932, one of four appearances as a Saint. He also scored a try and kicked three goals for England against Other Nationalities at Workington on 30 March 1933, although the home team lost 27-34. Jack was chosen for the 1936 tour Down Under and had some memorable clashes with the Aussie forward Ray Stehr. After a melee in the Second Test at Sydney, both were sent off and the band struck up 'Goodbye Sweetheart' in their honour!

A popular member of the Saints' Past Players' Hall of Fame, Jack was mine host at the Boilermakers Arms in Sutton for many years and passed away on 20 January 1990. His son John and grandson Chris also played for the Saints – a supreme rugby league dynasty.

Len Aston

Loose forward 1939-1950

Previous club: Junior rugby

St Helens debut: 9 December 1939 v. Broughton Rangers

Final St Helens appearance: 25 December 1950 v. Leigh

Appearances: 125

Tries: 26

Goals: 9

Points: 96

Transferred to: Retired

Representative honours: Lancashire, England, Great Britain

The Second World War denied a whole generation of rugby league fans from watching their idols and Len Aston was no exception. Although predominantly a soccer player in his youth, he played in a works rugby competition for Oldfield Recs at Knowsley Road in 1939 and impressed so much that he was signed up by the Saints' committee. After War service in India, Burma and Germany, Len was demobbed in 1946 and returned to Knowsley Road to rebuild his rugby career all over again.

Len first played as a centre but he was later switched to the pack where he became one of the most cultured second-rowers in the game. He had a meteoric rise to fame when selected for Great Britain in his first season as a regular first teamer at Knowsley Road. Indeed Aston and his teammate Jimmy Stott were the first post-war St Helens players to be selected for Great Britain. He was chosen for international football before county representation, a rapid rise indeed. The St Helens pair helped Britain defeat New Zealand 11-10 in the First Test at Headingley on 4 October 1947, with Aston scoring a try. He went on to make two further appearances for his country in the remaining Tests against the Kiwis during 1947/48. An England and Lancashire representative, Len made 116 appearances for his club from 1946/47 to 1950/51 and captained the Saints for a spell.

George Parsons, the Welsh second-row forward who joined St Helens in 1948 from Newport is in no doubt as to Len's unique football ability: 'He had this stop-start action, which Lewis Jones did later. Len would run up to the opposing forwards and stop dead. Then he would waggle his right leg and go through the eye of a needle.' At one stage deadly rivals Wigan were prepared to offer a virtual blank cheque to sign him, but Len was going nowhere.

Len had a mesmerising 'dummy' that he used to great effect, scoring a brilliant touchdown against Leigh in a Lancashire Cup tie at Knowsley Road in 1947 by totally bamboozling opposing defenders in a mazy fifty-yard run. Indeed, Len once sold the perfect dummy in a match at Knowsley Road – so good, in fact, that the referee Laurie Thorpe blew the whistle for a forward pass.

It was with great sadness that he was forced to give up the game prematurely, after tests revealed that he had an enlarged heart. There was no option for Len but to retire and he received a benefit match against Hull, on 3 March 1951. His Saints and international colleague Jimmy Stott kicked 6 goals and there were 9 scintillating tries, in front of a 12,000 crowd – enterprising attacking rugby which Len greatly appreciated.

Bob Atkin

Front-row forward 1922-1936

Previous club: Clock Face

St Helens debut: 16 December 1922 v. Keighley

Final St Helens appearance: 11 April 1936 v. Warrington

Appearances: 401

Tries: 9

Goals: 0

Points: 27

Transferred to: Retired

Representative honours: None

At a time when there were a large, almost disproportionate number of scrums in a match, sometimes numbering well into the seventies, the need for a solid front row was paramount for successful clubs. Bob Atkin was a real stalwart in the pack and one of the Saints' 400 Club, a fantastic achievement. Only George Lewis (428 appearances) and William Briers (515) played more times in the pre-Second World War era.

Signed from the Clock Face amateur club on 26 July 1922, Bob formed a dependable front-row combination with Bill Clarey, Lou Houghton and hooker Albert Simm. He was a member of the team that played against deadly rivals the Recs in the final of the Lancashire Cup at Warrington on 20 November 1926, his first major honour as a player.

The Saints became real contenders for major honours in the late twenties and early thirties. At the start of the 1929/30 campaign, the club stunned the rugby league world with the signing of three New Zealand internationals – Lou Hutt (front row), Roy Hardgrave (wing) and second-rower Trevor Hall. This meant that Atkin's opportunities were rather limited and he missed out on a place in the Wembley squad in 1930, against Widnes. Hutt and Hall had returned to New Zealand at the end of the 1930/31 campaign, however, giving the ever-loyal Atkin the chance to establish himself once again. This he duly did,

as the Saints lifted the Lancashire League trophy and stormed into the League Championship final after brushing aside Leeds' challenge in the semi-final at Knowsley Road. This was a real dogged affair, with Bob Atkin forming a formidable front row with fellow prop Ebor Hill and hooker Dave Cotton. Ben Halfpenny and Jack Arkwright were the second-rows, with the ever-dependable Walter Groves, a converted scrum-half, locking the scrum. Skipper George Lewis kicked three goals and Tom Winnard scored a superb try to bring the trophy home to Knowsley Road for the first time. Then it was back to Headquarters at the White Lion Hotel for the celebrations to begin in earnest.

Bob was in the front row for the 1932 Lancashire Cup final against Warrington at Wigan in front of over 28,000 spectators. The Saints were beaten 9-10 after a great struggle, but it was the last hurrah in terms of success until the early 1950s. The next few years saw the breaking up of the title-winning side, as extreme financial pressures forced the Saints to sell their biggest stars, including Alf Ellaby to Wigan and Bob's fellow packman, Jack Arkwright, to Warrington. Bob went on to play his last match against Warrington, on 11 April 1935, some seventeen years after he first signed, a great club man, who never let the Saints down.

Frank Barrow

Full-back 1961-1972

Previous club: Local juniors

St Helens debut: 7 January 1961 v. Warrington

Final St Helens appearance: 16 April 1972 v. Batley

Appearances: 233 + 11 subs

Tries: 13

Goals: 3

Points: 45

Transferred to: Leigh

Representative honours: Lancashire

Frankie Barrow was born and bred in Thatto Heath and attended the famous St Austins school, where he became a schoolboy star, like other famous old boys such as Alex Murphy and Austin Rhodes, and signed professional forms for his home-town club. Frank was a real crowd pleaser, a big-hearted player and utterly fearless, who would pick the ball up in the full-back position and get as far as he could, leaving a trail of dead and dying in his wake. In defence, too, he was equally enthusiastic and uncompromising, definitely a man to have in your side when the going got tough.

Frank became an established member of the side, following Kel Coslett's injury early in the 1964/65 campaign. His first winner's medal was in the 1964 Lancashire Cup final against Swinton, at Central Park and the honours just kept on coming! He played a major role in the 1966 Challenge Cup final, when rivals Wigan were comprehensively beaten 21-2. Frank played in three successive Championship Finals, from 1965-67 (including the replay in 1967) and also wore the No.1 jersey in the 24-12 defeat of Leeds in 1970. There were also two Floodlit finals and four Lancashire Cup final appearances: 1964, 1967 (plus replay) and 1970. Frank was highly rated by his teammates, and a good club man. The occasion never got to him,

no matter how big, and he was always enthusiastic and upbeat in the dressing room.

A Lancashire County representative at Knowsley Road, Frank joined Leigh in 1972, when he had graduated to the second row. He went on to win the Floodlit Trophy with the Hilton Park outfit, before retiring as a player, with thirteen major final appearances under his belt. Frank later coached Swinton and Oldham, together with a memorable spell as assistant to coach Mike McClennan at Knowsley Road. Frank also assisted Mike with Tonga in the 1995 World Cup. He is also revered in the amateur game for his work in resurrecting the Thatto Heath, Portico Panthers and Vine Tavern clubs – putting much back into the local community.

Frank's brothers, Tony and Billy also played for the Saints and all three of the Barrow brothers have had sons playing professionally, Tony Barrow with Swinton (Tony senior's son), Paul Barrow for Warrington and Swinton (Billy's son) and Stephen Barrow (Frank's son), for Wigan, Hull and London Broncos; a real family affair.

A bona-fide rugby league legend in every respect, Frankie was inducted into the Saints' Past Players' Hall of Fame in 2005 – a particularly poignant occasion. This was just months after Frank had fought his biggest battle, after contracting the potentially deadly bacterial infection septicaemia. Yet Frank beat the near-fatal illness, showing typical courage and resolve.

Tom Barton

Full-back, winger 1904-1921

Previous club: Local juniors

St Helens debut: 16 March 1904 v. Millom

Final St Helens appearance: 17 September 1921 v. Rochdale Hornets

Appearances: 226

Tries: 97

Goals: 118

Points: 527

Transferred to: Retired

Representative honours: England

Tom Barton was a real 'superstar' in the era before the First World War. He was a supremely talented footballer, who could play with equal power and skill in any position in the backs. He dominated a game; his tackling and kicking were superb. Apart from his tremendous strength, he had lightening pace over 120 yards. Yet his vigorous style of play and fiery temperament was often conducive to injury.

A former soccer player in his youth, Barton made his Saints' debut against Millom in March 1904, during the club's promotion season from the Second Division and made the full-back position his own when former Captain Tom Foulkes retired at the end of the campaign. Indeed, he was a surprise call-up for England in the rugby league international match against Other Nationalities at Central Park, Wigan, on 1 January 1906, following the late withdrawal of Halifax full-back Billy Little through injury.

The Saints enjoyed their best ever league finish in tenth place in 1909/10. Barton had been moved to the wing to accommodate New Zealand full-back Jum Turtill – who also took on the club captaincy. Although hampered by injury early on, he stormed back to find his best form, scoring 14 tries in his typical no-nonsense style, putting him in contention for a place in the first English team to tour Australasia in the summer of 1910. He was selected

yet did not go, because the rugby league would not make up his wages to his mother while he was away. There were no allowances for single men.

His soccer skills were also put to good use, when he went to America for a spell, in 1907, following his trade as a bricklayer. He signed up with New York Caledonians as a goalkeeper and enjoyed some success during his stay. He soon returned home to what he did best, however, terrorising opposing defences on the rugby league field.

Tom was still a potent force in the 1914/15 season, when he played in 30 matches, scoring 37 tries, plus 34 goals for good measure. He was captain of the team and responsible for preventing a threatened players' strike before the 1915 Challenge Cup final against Huddersfield at Watersheddings, when bonuses were not paid. Yet the Yorkshiremen posted a record 37-3 victory over their opponents. No-one deserved a medal more than Tommy Barton. One of the giants of the game in St Helens, he played on after the Great War, until he was over forty years of age, retiring after a couple of matches in 1921/22. He later worked overseas in Argentina, Chile and Brazil for a spell, before taking a job at the Triplex factory in St Helens. Tom remained a regular visitor to Knowsley Road for the rest of his life.

Billy Benyon
Centre 1961-1977

Previous club: Local juniors

St Helens debut: 10 March 1962 v. Rochdale Hornets

Final St Helens appearance: 1 January 1977 v. Warrington

Appearances: 509 + 5 subs

Tries: 154

Goals: 1

Points: 464

Transferred to: Warrington

Representative honours: Lancashire, England, Great Britain

Billy Benyon's record of achievement is quite staggering. He signed for the Saints on his sixteenth birthday in 1961 and during his sixteen years with the Knowsley Road club, he appeared in no fewer than twenty major finals, including three Wembley visits in 1966, 1972 and 1976. Yet it could all have been so different for the local lad who progressed through the 'C' and 'B' teams to first team level. Bill played for both St Helens and Lancashire Schoolboys in 1959 and the following year gained county honours at soccer. Future Liverpool captain Tommy Smith was in the same team. He had trials with Bolton Wanderers and West Bromwich Albion, but turned down an offer from the latter because he wanted to play rugby league.

Bill was given his debut in the home game against Rochdale Hornets at the back end of the 1961/62 season and on 27 October 1962, seventeen-year-old Benyon played in his first major final, as Swinton were defeated 7-4 in the Lancashire Cup final at Central Park. He played at stand-off, his preferred position at the start of his career, with Jeff Heaton, another 'young gun' filling in at scrum-half for Alex Murphy. A superb all-round footballer, with

great hands and a crunching tackle, Bill became a regular in the Saints' line-up as a centre in the 1964/65 campaign, when the team retained the Lancashire Cup final, yet lost out to Halifax in the Championship final at Swinton. He did have cartilage removed during this time, which blunted his effectiveness for several months. The following season saw the Saints lift four trophies; the League Leaders, Lancashire League, League Championship and Challenge Cup. At Wembley, against deadly rivals Wigan, Bill put in an astute grubber kick for his winger Len Killeen to dive over for Saints' second try virtually to seal the destiny of the trophy with a 14-2 score-line after fifty-four minutes. In the Championship final shortly after, he helped Len Killeen to go over for a hat-trick of tries in Saints' 35-12 victory over Halifax, to avenge the defeat of the previous campaign. By this time, Bill was playing on the left, with the switch of skipper Alex Murphy into the right centre berth.

Following Murphy's subsequent departure from Knowsley Road in 1967, Benyon went on to form a deadly partnership with winger Les Jones that

was to endure well into the next decade. Two more Lancashire Cup winner's medals followed, against Warrington (1967) and Oldham (1968), and Bill looked forward to even more glory in the years to come. Indeed, the Saints won back-to-back Championship finals at the start of the 1970s – an achievement comparable with anything in the club's history. After disposing of Leeds at Odsal in 1970, the Saints faced Wigan in the 1971 final at Swinton. As Wigan led 11-12 in the last two minutes, John Walsh attempted a drop-goal, which was badly sliced. The bounce beat winger Stuart Wright and was picked up by Benyon, who threw himself over the try-line for what commentator Eddie Waring described as a 'real grandstand finish!' Bill was really struggling with elbow and shoulder problems at the time and was promptly substituted by coach Jim Challinor before the final whistle.

Benyon was in his pomp in the early 1970s as a creative and strike centre. He scored over 20 tries and made over 40 appearances in 1969/70 and 1970/71 and was an established county player, with five Great Britain caps. Yet he missed out on both Australian tours in 1970 and 1974. He picked up his second Challenge Cup winner's medal after Saints' 16-13 defeat of Leeds in 1972, however, and enjoyed a successful testimonial in 1972. By now entering the veteran stage, he was an integral member of the side that won the First Division

Championship in 1975 by a staggering 11 points from second-placed Wigan.

The year 1976 was another great one for Benyon. He was a member of the famous 'Dad's Army' side that defeated Widnes at Wembley and, playing at stand-off half, helped to create the crucial first try for Eddie Cunningham after an incisive break. Bill won back-to-back Premiership finals in 1976 and 1977, captaining the side in the latter game, against Warrington and scoring a vital try in the 32-20 success – his twentieth final appearance as a Saint. He moved on to Warrington in October 1977 as player-coach, where he won the only medal missing from his career, in a John Player Trophy success against Widnes in 1978, at St Helens.

Billy returned to Knowsley Road as Coach in place of his former team-mate Kel Coslett, at the start of the 1982/83 campaign, and two years later led them to a Lancashire Cup and Premiership double, when Mal Meninga joined the club. Unfortunately, he was replaced halfway into the following campaign by Alex Murphy. Bill had further spells at Leigh and Swinton, before retirement. A member of the Saints' Past Players Hall of Fame, he made a total of 509 full appearances for the St Helens club, more than any other local-born three-quarter, third overall behind Kel Coslett and William Briers – a phenomenal achievement indeed!

Tommy Bishop
Scrum-half 1966-1969

Previous club: Barrow

St Helens debut: 29 January 1966 v. Halifax

Final St Helens appearance: 10 May 1969 v. Castleford

Appearances: 135

Tries: 47

Goals: 17

Points: 175

Transferred to: Cronulla (Australia)

Representative honours: Lancashire, Great Britain

Forever remembered as one of the great characters at Knowsley Road, Tommy Bishop's record as a player and coach – on two continents – has few equals. A typical rugby league scrum-half – tough, cheeky, pugnacious and skilful – at 5ft 7ins and eleven stone he was originally turned down by St Helens, his local team, because he was too small! Bishop began his league career with Blackpool Borough in the early sixties, and his gutsy, perpetual motion displays attracted the attention of Barrow, who bought him for £4,000 in 1964/65.

St Helens signed him in 1966 for £5,500 just before the cup register closed and he played so well that the great Alex Murphy was moved to right centre to accommodate him. His first game for the Saints, a Challenge Cup tie at Wakefield Trinity, showed his great enthusiasm for a scrap, as he scored a crucial try under the posts and led the visitors to victory on a real 'glue-pot' pitch. Tom helped his new club to a fantastic four-trophy haul by the end of the season – the Challenge Cup, League Championship, League Leader's Trophy and Lancashire League; success unparalleled in the history of the club. Bishop became an automatic choice for the Australian tour in 1966, making his Test debut against the Kangaroos at Sydney on

25 June alongside Cliff Watson and John Mantle. Although Britain lost the Ashes, the 'Mighty Atom' captured the hearts of the sporting public 'Down Under' with some exhilarating displays.

'Bish' won a total of fifteen caps for Great Britain and was appointed captain of the side for the French Tests in 1968/69, a season in which he also skippered his club and county. He helped St Helens to two further Lancashire League titles in 1966/67 and 1968/69 and gained two Lancashire Cup Winners medals in 1967/68 and 1968/69 before going to Australia to join the Cronulla club in the 1969 close season. The 'Sharks' were near the bottom of the Sydney competition, but within four years they were playing in the Grand Final, by which time the team included former Saints' prop Cliff Watson.

After just over five seasons at Cronulla, Bishop moved to Brisbane and Illawarra as a coach, then to North Sydney and finally back to Cronulla. Tom left after the 1980 season and returned to England to take up the coaching post at Workington, leading them to promotion in 1982. He had further stints at Leigh and Barrow and was the licensee of the Phoenix Arms in St Helens for a spell, before eventually settling in Australia once more. Paul, one of his three sons, played for the Saints against Wigan at Wembley in 1991, as a scrum-half, naturally – a real chip off the old block.

Scrum-half, loose forward 1934-1946

Previous club: Bradford Northern

St Helens debut: 3 December 1934 v. Barrow

Final St Helens appearance: 27 April 1946 v. Hull KR

Appearances: 230

Tries: 65

Goals: 0

Points: 195

Transferred to: Liverpool Stanley

Representative honours: None

Born and bred in Thatto Heath, Jack Bradbury played for the Saints in the somewhat less-than-heady days of the mid 1930s, and the war years, when the club was cash-strapped. Signed by the Saints from Bradford Northern on 2 November 1934, he began his career with the fledgling Wigan Highfield club. A strong, powerful player, Jackie was, at 5ft 8ins and twelve and a half stone, like whipcord. He was ideally a scrum-half, although he was deadly at loose forward, where he would frequently knock the stuffing out of opposing back-rowers and the scrum-half. Nothing seemed to bother him. Jack played above his strength and weight – he would give away as much as three stone when tackling the bigger forwards, but it made no difference; his opponent would usually hit the turf with an unceremonious thud. Jack had a real devilish streak in his play and he was well known to referees for his fiery temperament on the field.

By the late 1930s, however, rugby league was no longer flourishing in St Helens like it once did, and for the visit of Australia on Thursday 2 December 1937 they were met by a combined Saints-Recs XIII. Australia scored first, with a converted try, yet 'Jackie Brad' soon brought them back into contention, with a brilliant try from the base of the scrum, that was converted by his Saints' teammate Stan Powell. Australia went on to win by 15-7, although Bradbury had been the home side's most influential player by a mile. Jackie was quick over thirty yards and hard to stop close to the line.

He played as a guest for Eddie Waring's Dewsbury outfit in 1941, together with his Saints' teammates Les Garner, Jack Waring and Frank Tracey and picked up a Yorkshire Cup winner's medal in the 15-5 victory over Bradford Northern in 1941. Jim Sullivan also played full-back for Dewsbury in the same match.

A stalwart during Saints' first season back in competitive football after the war, Jack could still turn on the magic when he pulled on the boots, although he was officially the club's trainer-coach and well into his late thirties. He retained the ability to dictate play wherever he wanted 'marshalling his troops like Montgomery,' as one local journalist so succinctly put it, with darting breaks from the scrum-half position, that seemed to be too fast and sudden for his teammates.

Jack joined Liverpool Stanley as player-coach at the start of the 1946/47 campaign, when the St Helens club were still appealing for clothing coupons to buy more playing kit. A bricklayer by trade, who finished his working life at Pilkington's Ravenhead Works, Jack was quiet and unassuming off the field, bearing no relation to the fiery character on it.

William Briers
Forward 1895-1912

Previous club: St Helens Recreation

St Helens debut: 7 September 1895 v. Rochdale Hornets

Final St Helens appearance: 13 April 1912 v. Hunslet

Appearances: 515

Tries: 115

Goals: 0

Points: 345

Transferred to: Retired

Representative honours: Lancashire

In the early days of the Northern Union, the forwards mauled and scrimmaged to get the ball to the three-quarters who had the pace. Fast forwards were a rarity, but Saints had in their pack William Briers, a man with a reputation for strength and speed. 'Kitty' as he was known (he was 'kitty-pawed') could also do 100 yards in eleven seconds. He was also considered to be one of the greatest dribblers of a ball that the game has ever seen. Indeed he once scored a try against Runcorn by dribbling virtually the whole length of the field.

Born on 11 February 1875, Billy first played soccer, but he found that rugby was much too alluring and he began to play for his local club, Ravenhead St Johns. By the age of sixteen, he had joined the St Helens Recreation club and became a first team regular. After a couple of seasons at Boundary Road, he expressed a wish to join his pals Tom Foulkes and 'Ned' Ashcroft in the St Helens' town team and he duly became a Saint. When the Northern Union was formed in 1895/96, Briers decided to remain with the club and in the same season he gained his county cap, playing against Cheshire at Stockport and Yorkshire at Huddersfield. During the next five seasons, up

to and including the 1900/01 campaign, Billy represented the Red Rose shire in every one of their engagements. He was Lancashire captain during the 1901/02 season.

Billy was a member of the Saints' team in the very first Challenge Cup final in 1897, at Headingley, when they were defeated 10-3 by the powerful 'Gallant Youths' of Batley. When Oldham visited Knowsley Road on 1 October 1898 they did so as reigning champions of Lancashire. Their supporters gave Saints no earthly chance. They would be beaten out of sight with consummate ease. How wrong they were. The scintillating Saints tore the Cotton Spinners to shreds by 15-9. It was a magnificent team performance and a personal triumph for 'Kitty' Briers. Showing his versatility by playing as a half-back he roared in for three tries – a magnificent individual performance. To their credit, a stunned Oldham side accepted defeat like true gentlemen. They later presented Briers with a special cap to mark his achievement, and got their revenge later in the season to the tune of 16-0. On 29 April 1900, he was also a member of the side that beat Runcorn in extra time to lift the South West Lancashire and Border Towns Cup at Widnes – the first honour won by the Saints in Northern Union football.

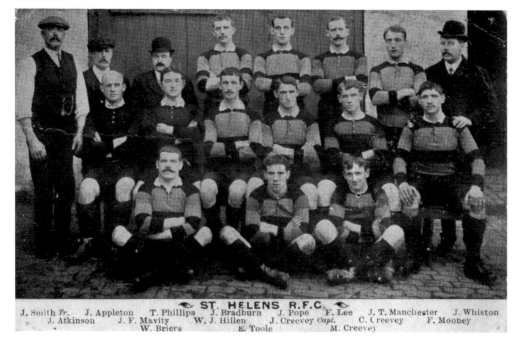

ST. HELENS R.F.C.

J. Smith *Tr.*　J. Appleton　T. Phillips　J. Bradburn　J. Pope　F. Lee　J. T. Manchester　J. Whiston
J. Atkinson　J. F. Mavity　W. J. Hillen　J. Creevey *Capt.*　C. Creevey　F. Mooney
W. Briers　E. Toole　M. Creevey

When his pal Tommy Foulkes retired from the game in 1904, it was Briers who took over the captaincy for several years. At just over even time, Briers was a speedy customer and Foulkes often spoke of the times that they took many a bright sovereign from visiting teams and spectators when they wanted to back their opinion that Briers couldn't do it! Billy was only sent off once in his career, by an over-officious and inexperienced referee, for a quite innocuous offence – but it greatly troubled Billy for some time afterwards.

After the last match of the 1911/12 season, at Hunslet, Billy Briers announced his retirement. He was the last playing member left from the team which had defeated Rochdale in the club's first Northern Union match in 1895. The lad from Thatto Heath had played in nearly ninety per cent of Saints' matches between 1895 and 1912. He made over 500 appearances for St Helens – one of only four Saints' players to do so, scoring 114 tries. An ever-present in 1896/97 and 1908/09, he appeared in 78 consecutive matches from November 1907 to February 1910. A beneficiary in 1907/08, he played nineteen times for Lancashire, captaining them twice; although an international cap eluded him.

Kitty owed his tremendous consistency to a high level of fitness. He possessed a great turn of speed and had tremendous shoulder muscles for his size. These were developed during his years at Lea Green Colliery, where he was a Blacksmith's striker. A quiet, steady fellow, Briers never gave up his interest in St Helens football. Every Saturday he could be seen in his favourite place in the stand, white moustached, gravely smoking his beloved pipe, seldom commenting either favourably or unfavourably on play or players. He was to die tragically at the age of fifty-six after an operation for appendicitis in the early 1930s. His brother, Ben, also played for the Saints in the 1920s.

During the Saints' Past Players' Dinner in 2003, the Saints' Heritage Society presented a silver salver to each member of the Saints' 500 Club – Eric Chisnall, Bill Benyon, Kel Coslett and Billy Briers. A close relative, Tom Cheetham, represented Billy Briers, and showed the large audience of several hundred Billy's county cap and 1897 Challenge Cup medal. They broke into warm and sustained applause – a magnificent tribute to one of Saints' all-time great players.

Frank Carlton
Winger 1952-1960

Previous club: Parr Central School

St Helens debut: 6 April 1953 v. Huddersfield

Final St Helens appearance: 21 September 1960 v. Swinton

Appearances: 156

Tries: 129

Goals: 0

Points: 378

Transferred to: Wigan

Representative honours: Lancashire, England, Great Britain

Frank Carlton's name is forever enshrined in the history of the Saints as being the man who broke the deadlock with a super try in the 1956 Challenge Cup final against Halifax, enabling St Helens to lift the coveted trophy for the first time! Vince Karalius picked up a loose ball and put Brian Howard away. The young centre beat one man, drew winger Daniels and swept the ball out to the left. Frank Carlton took the pass and swerved effortlessly past full-back Griffiths just beyond halfway. A tremendous burst of speed saw him leave the desperate Halifax cover trailing in his wake, as he touched down near the posts, to one of the biggest roars ever heard at Wembley.

Although he was a town and county representative at rugby league during his schooldays, he signed amateur forms for Everton at the age of fifteen after leaving the famous Parr Central High School, playing regularly in the Colts team. Injury hindered his progress and he returned to the local leagues. Yet he was still in demand as a result of his rugby exploits and he was persuaded by chairman Harry Cook to sign for the Saints in October 1952.

Once established in the first team, his pace and finishing ability tormented the tightest of defences.

Frank was Saints' leading try-scorer on three occasions, his most prolific performance coming in the 1955/56 campaign, with 40 tries, including three hat-tricks, together with a stunning four-try performance in the 53-6 demolition of Bradford Northern in the third round of the Challenge Cup. He played in the 44-2 thrashing of the 1956 Australian tourists at Knowsley Road and despite a season hindered by injury in 1957/58, he was selected for the Australasian tour. Although he only played in one Test Down Under, in New Zealand, he scored 20 tries in 8 appearances overall.

Things were not easy for Frank after the tour, with Tom van Vollenhoven a permanent fixture on the right flank. This was further complicated with the signing of another South African, Jan Prinsloo – a left winger. Both Prinsloo and Carlton were used to finance the world record £11,000 deal that saw Wigan's Mick Sullivan arrive at Knowsley Road, with Frank going in the other direction!. How ironic that he would face his former teammates in the Challenge Cup final later in the season and end up on the losing side.

Frank went on to make his second Australian tour in 1962 and played in his third Challenge Cup final, for Wigan against Wakefield Trinity, in 1963 – his second loser's medal. A tremendously popular figure at Knowsley Road and a real gentleman, Frank is a worthy member of the Saints' Past Players' Association Hall of Fame.

Eric Chisnall

Second row, front-row forward 1966-1982

Previous club: Local juniors

St Helens debut: 18 March 1967 v. Huddersfield

Final St Helens appearance: 21 February 1982 v. York

Appearances: 496 + 27 subs

Tries: 70

Goals: 0

Points: 210

Transferred to: Leigh

Representative honours: Lancashire, England, Great Britain

One of Saints' all-time great forwards, Eric Chisnall had trials at Wigan as a youngster, but eventually signed for his home-town club from Pilkington Recs in December 1966. A durable and skilful footballer, Eric became a member of the exclusive Saints' 500 Club – the elite band who have made over 500 appearances for the club, together with his teammates Kel Coslett and Bill Benyon, and William 'Kitty' Briers, a forward from before the First World War. Eric had two brothers who also played professional rugby – Dave, who spent most of his career at Warrington, but also came to play with Eric at Knowsley Road, and Les, who was on Leigh's books.

Eric burst onto the scene with his strong running, yet he showed great presence of mind with his first try for the club, in the replayed Lancashire Cup final against Warrington in 1967, when he picked up from acting half-back and plunged over the line – a crucial try – breaking the 8-8 deadlock. The Saints won 13-10, with skipper Tom van Vollenhoven holding the trophy aloft. Eric was beginning to carve out a reputation for himself as a hard-running second rower, racing into gaps and leaving the opposition for dead. He was soon an ever-present in the team and, at times, the only local-born player in the pack.

Chisnall picked up his second Lancashire Cup winner's medal after the defeat of Oldham in 1968, when he roared in for a typically spectacular individual try in Saints' 30-2 success. He could also off-load in the tackle, a skill of immense value during the era of the four-tackle rule, superbly illustrated in a cameo from the 1970 Championship final victory against Leeds at Odsal. Coslett worked a dummy run-around with Jeff Heaton before sending John Mantle storming through the gap. He fed Chisnall, who carried on the move, drawing three defenders before a perfectly timed one-handed pass found Frank Myler, who put hooker Bill Sayer over near the posts. Eric's cover tackling was also in evidence that afternoon, as it was the following year, when the Saints retained the trophy by beating Wigan at Swinton, when the forwards – minus John Mantle – had to endure a tremendous onslaught in the second half.

Eric represented his county on four occasions and played twice for Lancashire during the 1971/72 campaign – an incredibly gruelling season when he played in over fifty matches for his club, including half in the front row as the Saints triumphed in the BBC Trophy and Challenge

Cup final. Eric had a blinder at Wembley against Leeds, running out wide and sending a precision pass out to Les Jones, who scored Saints' second try to extend the lead they never relinquished. Eric's reputation as a fine all-round player had its rewards with selection for the 1974 Australasian tour squad, where he played in eighteen matches, including two Tests against Australia and New Zealand. Eric scored a fine try in the Second Test against Australia in Sydney, which Great Britain won 16-11, although they lost the rubber 2-1.

Eric was back to his best form during the 1974/75 season, when his 12 tries in 41 matches helped the Saints to the First Division Championship, some nine points ahead of second-placed Wigan. Indeed, the glory trail for Eric and the Saints continued the following season, as the BBC Floodlit Trophy, Challenge Cup and Premiership Trophy all came to Knowsley Road. Twenty-nine-year-old Eric was one of the younger members of the famous 'Dad's Army' team at Wembley against Widnes and he stamped his authority on the Premiership final clash with Salford by weaving past three hapless defenders before planting the ball down for the try that clinched Saints' 13-2 success. Twelve months later, he played in his second successive Premiership

final, where Warrington were well beaten 32-20 at Swinton. He had, by this time, been joined by his brother Dave at Knowsley Road – a burly front-rower who had toured Australia in 1970.

Eric was a real tough customer, who generally managed to avoid serious injury during his career at Knowsley Road; yet he fractured his forearm and dislocated his wrist against Dewsbury in 1977 and was forced to miss the 1978 Challenge Cup final, where his power in the pack was sorely missed. As the Saints' glory team of the 1970s gradually dispersed, Eric remained loyal to the cause and played through to the 1981/82 season as Saints rebuilt their team around a nucleus of young local talent. He adopted the role as 'Elder Statesman' of the pack alongside George Nicholls as they nurtured the young lads in the team. Although his pace had declined somewhat, he was able to compensate with his superb handling skills and still generated tremendous respect from his teammates. Eric eventually joined Leigh for £13,000 in March 1982, signalling the end of a magnificent career in the red vee for a genuine Knowsley Road great. A member of the Saints' Past Players' Hall of Fame, Eric continued to give youngsters the value of his vast experience by assisting with the running of the Under-16s at Knowsley Road in 2005.

Bill Clarey
Front-row forward 1919-1930

Previous club: Thatto Heath

St Helens debut: 4 October 1919 v. Widnes

Final St Helens appearance: 4 October 1930 v. Dewsbury

Appearances: 252

Tries: 13

Goals: 0

Points: 41

Transferred to: Retired

Representative honours: None

In those far-off days between the wars, rugby was thriving in St Helens, with the town team vying for honours against the Pilkington Works team – the St Helens Recs. It was in this competitive environment that Bill Clarey joined the Saints from Thatto Heath junior rugby. He made his first team debut against Widnes on 4 October 1919 and remained a regular for the next eleven years. A solid reliable front-rower, adept at scrummaging, Bill played in a side that struggled on and off the field in the first few years of the 1920s, when the club frequently found itself short of money, with success seemingly as far away as ever.

By the 1924/25 campaign, however, the team was developing into one capable of challenging for major honours. Inspired by the sensational form of newly discovered wing sensation Alf Ellaby, the Saints reached the County Cup final in 1926/27, where they played against their deadly rivals Recs at Warrington in front of almost 20,000 fans at Wilderspool. The tackling from both packs of forwards was quite uncompromising, with Clarey at one stage lying in the mud motionless for several minutes before he was revived by the famous 'magic sponge'. Tries from Ellaby and Fairclough gave the Saints a sensational 10-2 success, with Clarey rubbing the back of his head after the match.

Revenge was in the air during the Championship play-off at City Road, when Recs and Saints went head-to-head once more. This was to be very much the Recs' day, in a 33-0 mauling, where the visiting pack got more and more rattled. Just after half-time, Clarey traded punches with Recs' second-rower Tommy Smith, triggering an all-in brawl, with the result that three players were sent off (the two original protagonists miraculously escaped the wrath of referee Revd Frank Chambers).

The signing of star New Zealand front-rower Lou Hutt restricted Bill's appearances during the 1929/30 campaign. He was now thirty, and ten years in the 'engine room' of the pack had started to take its toll. Yet he was selected in the Saints' team for the crucial Challenge Cup semi-final replay against Wigan at Leigh's Mather Lane ground. It was a triumph for the Saints' three-quarters, who destroyed the opposition with four tries to two from a steady stream of possession supplied by hooker Bill Clarey. Bill played in the final at Wembley against Widnes, but came away with a loser's medal as the Saints – for a variety of reasons – failed to hit top form and lost 10-3 in one of the competition's great upsets. Although Bill retired soon after the game, he had more than played his part in one of the most famous eras in the history of St Helens Rugby League Club.

Gary Connolly
Full-back, centre 1988-1993

Previous club: Blackbrook

St Helens debut: 22 January 1989 v. Hull KR

Final St Helens appearance: 16 May 1993 v. Wigan

Appearances: 128 + 5 subs

Tries: 46

Goals: 0

Points: 184

Transferred to: Wigan

Representative honours: England, Great Britain

Local-born Gary Connolly was already a schoolboy star when he signed for the Saints as a seventeen-year-old. Such was his ability that coach Alex Murphy virtually put him straight into the first team for his debut, against Hull KR on 22 January 1989. Confident and composed, the young full-back immediately impressed with his sheer speed, safe hands and tremendous tackling technique, courtesy of supreme upper body strength. Indeed, one of his finest matches was just a couple of months later, in the rugby league Challenge Cup semi-final against a powerful Widnes outfit at Central Park, when Saints triumphed 16-14 with a real backs-to-the-wall performance. Although there was to be disappointment for the youngster in the final against Wigan, Gary soon made the No.1 jersey his own over the next season, with Australian Phil Veivers moving into the centres.

Despite a second Wembley disappointment two years later, also against the 'old enemy', Gary's ambition for silverware was fulfilled in 1991/92, with a 24-10 success over Rochdale Hornets in the Lancashire Cup final at Wilderspool. Coach Mike McLennan had moved Connolly into the centres and he formed a potent three-quarter line, with the likes of Hunte, Sullivan, Ropati and Loughlin. The team finished as runners-up

in the First Division and hoped to provide a credible challenge to Wigan in the forthcoming campaign. Meanwhile, Gary's sparkling form had been recognised at international level and he was selected for the Australasian tour in the summer of 1992, alongside teammates Hunte, Loughlin and Nickle. Later that year he would also feature in the Great Britain side that was defeated so narrowly by Australia at Wembley in the World Cup final.

Gary gave one of his finest all-round displays in the Boxing Day match against Wigan at Knowsley Road in 1992, ending in a famous 41-6 triumph for the home side. Although the Saints eventually lost the First Division title on points difference, there was some consolation at Old Trafford, when Wigan were defeated 10-4 in a tense Premiership final. Gary scored a crucial first-half try by scooping up a loose ball and plunging over the line. This proved to be his last for the club as he had been offered a significant wage increase to join the team that had denied him in so many competitions to date – Wigan. Within a couple of years he had won every honour in the game and his departure left a gaping hole in the Saints' future team-building plans.

Always an extremely durable footballer, Gary continued to play into the twenty-first century in the Wigan three-quarter line as they challenged for honours in the Super League era. In the twilight of his career Gary had playing spells with Leeds Rhinos and Widnes Vikings.

Shane Cooper

Stand-off, loose forward 1987-1995

Previous club: Mangere East (New Zealand)

St Helens debut: 18 October 1987 v. Leigh

Final St Helens appearance: 7 May 1995 v. Halifax

Appearances: 269 + 2 subs

Tries: 76

Goals: 6

Points: 310

Transferred to: Widnes

Representative honours: New Zealand

Shane Cooper was a superb rugby league player – a great leader, with silky handling skills and a real master tactician who had the ability to read a game to perfection. He was also an uncompromising tackler and extremely durable, rarely missing a match during his distinguished career at Knowsley Road. A native of Auckland, where he starred with Mount Albert and Mangere East, Shane won a dozen Test caps for New Zealand, including a place on the substitute's bench for the 1988 World Cup final against Australia.

Essentially a playmaking replacement for the departed Harry Pinner, Shane started at scrum-half, but reverted to stand-off and Saints' coach Alex Murphy soon made him captain of the side. His tactical awareness and influence were much in evidence after just a few months at the helm when he led the team to victory in the 1988 John Player Trophy final at Central Park, Wigan; when a superb defensive display produced a fantastic 15-14 success against favourites Leeds. Quicker in thought, rather than pure pace, Shane joined the likes of Ellaby, Llewellyn, Myler and van Vollenhoven by scoring six tries in a match, against Hull in 1988 – a veritable master-class of support play in Saints' 64-2 victory. Indeed, the team were in contention for the First Division title, but buckled when Shane returned to New Zealand, achieving the runners-up spot behind Widnes.

The 1988/89 campaign was disastrous for Shane and the Saints, with the side finishing in seventh place in the League and whitewashed at Wembley in the Challenge Cup final by Wigan – Shane's darkest hour at Knowsley Road. He was still a major influence, however, and the Saints were back at Wembley in 1991, after a brilliant semi-final success over favourites Widnes. Once again, Saints fell at the final hurdle as Wigan triumphed 13-8.

By the early 1990s, the Saints still looked the most likely side to challenge Wigan, with loose forward Cooper forming a fabulous midfield triangle with Paul Bishop and hooker Paul Groves. He captained the side in their 1991 Lancashire Cup final success against Rochdale Hornets and there was further glory ahead as the Saints finished joint top of the First Division in 1993, beaten only on points difference by Wigan. Shane led the side to victory against the same opponents in the Premiership final at Old Trafford. Unfortunately, the success of the 1992/93 campaign was not consolidated. Although Shane was always a key figure in the team, further honours never materialised and he joined Widnes at the end of the 1994/95 campaign, steering the Chemics to the Challenge Cup semi-final against eventual winners St Helens. Shane was a great character, who always led by example and he remains one of the club's most influential captains.

Kel Coslett
Full-back, loose forward 1962-1976

Previous club: Aberavon RUFC (Wales)

St Helens debut: 18 August 1962 v. Salford

Final St Helens appearance: 22 May 1976 v. Salford

Appearances: 519 + 12 subs

Tries: 45

Goals: 1,639

Points: 3,413

Transferred to: Rochdale Hornets

Honours: Wales, Other Nationalities

Kel Coslett's achievements are phenomenal! He made the most appearances in the red and white jersey (519), kicked the most goals (1,639) and scored more points than any other Saint (3,413). Kel was the original Captain Fantastic, whose influence at loose forward was almost all-embracing in the golden era of the 1970s, calling the moves and handling all kicking duties. Born in Llanelli, Kel was a fly-half as a schoolboy and represented his county and country at that level. He was also a youth international and played with distinction for Llanelli and Aberavon, at one stage holding the Aberavon points-in-season record of 186. An ever-present in the 1961/62 Five Nations Championship at full-back, he became a Saint in July 1962, making his debut against Salford on 18 August at the Willows in a Western Championship game. The Saints won 35-24, with twenty-year old Coslett kicking four goals. A deadly marksman with the boot, Kel led the League's goal-kicking charts in his first season with 156 – a feat he was to achieve in both the 1970/71 and 1971/72 seasons. In his first season with the Saints, he only failed to score in one match, at home to Featherstone, on 20 April 1963.

Early in the 1964/65 campaign, however, a fractured ankle saw Frankie Barrow settle into the full-back role and South African Len Killeen given responsibility for goal-kicking. Yet Kel switched to loose forward and only a hip injury ruled him out of the Challenge Cup final against Wigan in 1966. By 1967/68 he had become a great ball handler and tactical kicker, who could read a game superbly. His influence was paramount during the 1970 Championship final against Leeds at Odsal, when the Saints won a magnificent 24-12 victory over their Yorkshire rivals. Twelve months later, Coslett held the trophy aloft as captain after a thrilling last-minute success over Wigan at Station Road, Swinton. It was one of the greatest games of his career and his brilliant touchline conversion of Bob Blackwood's try with four minutes to go set up a thrilling finale when the injured 'One-armed bandit' Billy Benyon scored a sensational last-minute try to seal a magnificent back-to-back success for the twelve-man Saints, who had had John Mantle sent off.

The 1971/72 season saw Coslett at the height of his powers as a captain and goal-kicker supreme. He kicked a club record haul of 214 goals in 54 matches and led the Saints to success in the Challenge Cup final against Leeds at Wembley.

This was really a 'tale of two kickers', as Coslett booted over four goals and a towering drop-goal that soared over the height of the posts at Wembley – some kick indeed. Leeds' kicker Terry Clawson, by contrast, had a nightmare with the boot. Yet it was Coslett's all-round performance and captaincy that earned him the coveted Lance Todd Trophy.

The Saints of 1975 won the First Division Championship at a canter, some eleven points ahead of second-placed Wigan, losing only three matches during the campaign, with Coslett's 129 goals (second in the charts behind Hull KR's Neil Fox) a key factor. By the 1975/76 season, Kel had given over the place-kicking duties to full-back Geoff Pimblett, to lighten the load somewhat. Beginning with a Floodlit Trophy success against Dewsbury at Knowsley Road, the side battled to the Challenge Cup final, where they faced a much younger Widnes side at a sweltering Wembley Stadium. Coslett had by this time graduated to the front row, which also included hooker Tony Karalius and John Mantle – a combined age of ninety-nine. Yet 'Dad's Army' refused to buckle and scored a crucial early try courtesy of Eddie Cunningham and never surrendered the lead, registering an amazing 20-5 victory. For Kel it was, quite simply, the hardest game of his life as he recovered backstage in the dressing room

from the effects of dehydration. The Saints had also battled to the Premiership final, against First Division Champions Salford and the 'Dad's Army' spirit lifted them once more to a 15-2 success over the powerful Red Devils. Kel led his team Down Under for a ground-breaking tour of Australia and New Zealand, including a match against Eastern Suburbs at the Sydney Cricket Ground, before moving to Rochdale Hornets as player-coach for the start of the 1976/77 campaign – the end of a remarkable fourteen-year career at Knowsley Road.

Kel played his last competitive match at the end of the 1978/79 season and coached Wigan for a spell before moving back to Knowsley Road in June 1980. It was a time of rebuilding at the club and Kel was sacked in May 1982 and replaced by Bill Benyon, but he had done a good job in difficult circumstances. A seasoned international for Wales, making twelve appearances from 1968-1975, Kel also coached the team from 1977-1982. He later returned once more to Knowsley Road as football manager and shared in the Super League triumphs of the club at the turn of the century. A member of the Saints' Past Players' Hall of Fame, Kel remains a popular and indeed legendary figure at Knowsley Road. The place would not be the same without him.

Charlie Crooks
Full-back 1919-1930

Previous club: Junior rugby

St Helens debut: 6 September 1919 v. Oldham

Final St Helens appearance: 3 May 1930 v. Widnes

Appearances: 290

Tries: 23

Goals: 19

Points: 107

Transferred to: Retired

Representative honours: Lancashire

Local-born Charlie Crooks was a real stalwart of the St Helens club, although he could have been lost to the code, having had soccer trials with Liverpool Football Club in his youth. Charlie played at stand-off on his debut in 1919 and also featured in the centre and on the wing, before settling down as first-choice full-back on the retirement of Saints' legend Tommy Barton. Charlie was a capable footballer, naturally strong and solid in the tackle, with a good kicking game – ideal for the No.1 jersey. Indeed, Charlie captained the side for a spell in the early 1920s before the arrival of Welshman George Lewis.

By the 1926/27 season, chairman Jim May had assembled a side capable of challenging for major honours, with local-born stars like winger Alf Ellaby and stand-off Les Fairclough drawing huge crowds to Knowsley Road. Charlie was a member of the side that defeated neighbours Recs in the 1926 Lancashire Cup final at Wilderspool. Over 19,000 rain-soaked spectators witnessed a particular feature of the game in those days, with full-backs Crooks and Dingsdale involved in several kicking duels. Tries by Ellaby and Fairclough, together with two goals from George Lewis ,gave St Helens their first-ever County Cup success.

The Saints were Lancashire League Champions in 1929/30, with the prospect of more silverware to come, especially when Wigan were beaten 22-10 in the Challenge Cup semi-final replay at Mather Lane, Leigh, when Crooks outshone Wigan's mighty full-back and captain Jim Sullivan. Yet the promise of riches untold gradually started to evaporate, as Leeds defeated the Saints 6-10 in a Championship Play-Off clash at Knowsley Road and Widnes pulled off one of the greatest Challenge Cup shocks of all time with a 10-3 success at Wembley. Charlie always recounted the poor preparation that led to Saints' Cup demise, including a visit to the Houses of Parliament on the Friday evening before the match, returning at well past one.

Charlie had persistent knee trouble during his career and announced his retirement after the cup final – an unfortunate end to the playing days of one of the Saints' most durable footballers. He was then thirty-three years of age and could not guarantee full fitness. Without peer at club level, Charlie faced stiff competition from Rochdale's Walter Gowers and Tommy Dingsdale for a Lancashire spot, although he scored a memorable 'kick and chase' try for the Red Rose county as they defeated rivals Yorkshire in the game at Oldham in 1924, on their way to the County Championship. Charlie also kicked a goal as Lancashire thrashed New Zealand at Leigh in 1927. A local newsagent and confirmed bachelor, who maintained a strong interest in the fortunes of the club for the rest of his life, Charlie Crooks was a Saint through and through.

Eddie Cunningham
Centre, second-row forward 1975-1979

Previous club: Wigan

St Helens debut: 9 February 1975 v. Bramley

Final St Helens appearance: 13 May 1979 v. Salford

Appearances: 132 + 9 subs

Tries: 75

Goals: 0

Points: 225

Transferred to: Leeds

Representative honours: Lancashire, Wales, Great Britain

A local lad, Eddie Cunningham played junior football in St Helens before joining Wigan in August 1969 and quickly established himself as a first team regular. Eddie was substitute for the Riversiders in the 1971 Championship final and played at loose forward during Wigan's Lancashire Cup success over Salford in 1973. He could play with equal effectiveness in the second row or in the centre, which is why the Saints signed him for a bargain £5,000 in 1975. Eddie was substitute in Saints'1975 Premiership final clash with Leeds, but produced a splendid display when he came on in the second half. A stocky, powerful man, he had the ability to burst out of tackles, when it seemed he must be held or dragged to the ground. His deceptive pace did the rest.

Eddie played in the centre during the famous 'Dad's Army' victory over Widnes at Wembley in 1976 and scored the crucial first try as the Saints went on to run their much younger opponents off their feet. Eddie was in top form as the Saints lifted the Premiership title in 1977, scoring a brilliant individual forty-yard solo try in the 32-20 success. Yet it was in the 1977/78 campaign that Eddie really came into his own, with his devastating strength and surging runs a major feature of the Saints' attacking machine. He finished the campaign third in the League's try-scoring charts with 30 touchdowns, with Stuart Wright (Widnes) and Keith Fielding (Salford) above him. Yet he was to face disappointment in the Challenge Cup final

at Wembley as Leeds ground their way to a 14-12 victory; an unfortunate end to a season that promised so much.

Eddie represented Lancashire and was selected for the Welsh World Championship squad in 1975 (his grandmother was Welsh), making his debut in the famous 12-7 victory over England in Brisbane, where he operated in the second row. Overall he played eight times for the Dragons and made one appearance for Great Britain, against Australia at Wigan in 1978, when the home side were unlucky to lose by just six points.

A £25,000 fee took him to Leeds in October 1979, but he soon returned to Lancashire with Widnes, where he made two more Challenge Cup final appearances; at Wembley in the 18-9 success over Hull KR in 1981 and winning the Lance Todd Trophy twelve months later in the drawn final against Hull, scoring two fine tries. Eddie had a spell at Batley before retiring from the game in the mid 1980s.

Eddie comes from a famous rugby family, with younger brothers Tommy (Saints and Warrington) and Keiron (Saints) – both hookers – who also went on to wear the scarlet jersey of the Principality. Amazingly, Keiron was not yet born when Eddie played in the 1976 Challenge Cup final.

Keiron Cunningham
Hooker 1994-

Previous club: Wigan St Judes

St Helens debut: 22 August 1994 v. Warrington

Appearances: 331 + 9 subs

Tries: 141

Goals: 0

Points: 564

Transferred to:

Representative honours: Lancashire, Wales, Great Britain

After over a decade of almost total success, Keiron Cunningham has joined Alf Ellaby and Alex Murphy as the greatest home-grown players to represent the St Helens club. His achievements are legendary and he is highly respected by teammates and opponents alike, including the Australian 'great' Gorden Tallis, who rated him as one of the top two players in the world. As an acting half-back, he has few equals. Supremely confident, he dominates the ruck area and is a blind-side specialist. Keiron has the ability to pick up the ball on the move, using his momentum and power to pierce the first line of defence. Indeed, his bull-like strength makes him virtually impossible to stop close to the line, as he invariably sets his sixteen-stone frame low and crashes over, taking several hapless defenders with him. Keiron developed the role further in the 2004 and 2005 campaigns, with lateral running and delayed passes from acting half-back, which caused further pandemonium for opposing defences. Add pace and terrific tackling ability and it is easy to see why he is so highly rated in the modern game.

Keiron is one of ten children, born in Thatto Heath on 28 October 1976, some five months after his brother Eddie won a Challenge Cup winner's medal for Saints against Widnes. His rise was quite meteoric and by the first season of Super League, in 1996, when he won the Young Player of the Year

award, he was already one of the most accomplished players in the competition. Indeed, his record of achievement for his home-town club is quite staggering: Man of the Match in the 1995/96 Regal Trophy final versus Wigan at the McAlpine Stadium; won four Challenge Cups (1996, 1997, 2001 and 2004) and four Super League Championships (1996, 1999, 2000 and 2002) with the Saints; named as a member of the mythical Super League Dream Team in 1996, 2000, 2001, 2002 and 2005; scored the most tries by a St Helens forward (141 by 2005); along with Chris Joynt, he has played in and won more Challenge Cup finals for St Helens than any other player – (5 finals, 4 wins). Keiron's tries in the 1996 and 2001 Challenge Cup finals ensure that he joins three other players who have scored tries in more than one Challenge Cup final for the club – Steve Llewellyn (1953 and 1956), Tommy Martyn (1997 and 2001) and Paul Sculthorpe (2002 and 2004). A natural rugby league player, he turned down a big-money deal from the Welsh RFU in 2001 to remain in the code that has brought him so much success.

Keiron has made seventeen appearances for Great Britain, including selection for the 1996 tour of Papua New Guinea and New Zealand and the 1999 Tri-Nations tournament in Australia. Yet he is proud of his Welsh roots and was a member of the 1995 and 2000 World Cup Squads, making eight appearances for the Principality overall. He also captained the side from the loose forward position against England at Wrexham in 2001. Keiron was in superb form during the 2005 Tri-Nations Tournament, although he has had more than his share of injuries during his career. Perhaps the worst came at the end of 2002, in the First Test against the Kiwis at Blackburn, when Keiron's elbow was so badly damaged that he had to have a total reconstruction of the joint. After pioneering surgery by Dr Stanley in Sheffield, he was able to resume his career, but it was touch and go.

Very much a self-effacing family man, Keiron has had such an influence on the Saints' team over the years that it is difficult to pick out individual highlights. According to the man himself, there are five magical moments that are the pick of the bunch. Number one: winning the World Club Challenge 20-18 against Brisbane Broncos in 2001 is the highlight of his career, having worked so hard in pre-season to achieve this particular goal. Number two: Keiron's first team debut, in the intimidating setting of the old Warrington ground at Wilderspool, surrounded by some of the players he had previously idolised from the terraces. Number three: the 1996 Challenge Cup final victory over Bradford Bulls, with Keiron scoring the first try of Saints' famous come-back victory after being 26-12 down. Number four: the Great Britain tour and his international debut against Papua New Guinea at Lae, on 28 September 1996, when he scored a try in Great Britain's 48-6 success – hot and humid, with 15,000 fans crammed into the small stadium. Number five: the 1996 Regal Trophy final against Wigan, when Keiron won his first Man of the Match award, providing a tantalising glimpse of what we were to enjoy over the next ten years. Indeed, Keiron enjoyed a successful testimonial in 2004, which included a memorable 32-16 victory over Wigan in the Challenge Cup final at the Millennium Stadium, Cardiff – another fabulous career highlight. He was also the natural choice to captain the side in the absence of Paul Sculthorpe in the latter part of the 2005 campaign – quite simply irreplaceable.

Bob Dagnall
Hooker 1959-1967

Previous club: Rochdale Hornets

St Helens debut: 5 March 1960 v. Warrington

Final St Helens appearance: 27 March 1967 v. Swinton

Appearances: 209 + 1 sub

Tries: 8

Goals: 0

Points: 24

Transferred to: Retired

Representative honours: Lancashire, Great Britain

During the early to mid-1960s, when the Saints were one of the most powerful outfits in the game, Thatto Heath-born Bob Dagnall wore the No.9 jersey with distinction. His schooldays were spent at Grange Park School, where he was first choice hooker. Yet two of his classmates went on to hook in the professional code – Frank McCabe (Saints) and Frank Platt (Wigan). The young Dagnall made a name for himself with the junior team Vine Tavern and signed for Rochdale Hornets in 1949/50, where there was a strong contingent of St Helens-born players, such as scrum-half Johnny Fishwick – who became a life-long friend and working colleague. Dagnall spent ten years at Rochdale, reaching the 1958 Challenge Cup semi-final only to lose to eventual winners Wigan.

Saints brought him home for the start of the 1959/60 campaign, however, and they were able to add his hooking, tackling and terrific ball-handling skills to one of the most formidable forward packs in the League, including names such as Terry, Vines, Watson, Huddart and Vince Karalius.

St Helens beat Wigan at Wembley in the 1961 Challenge Cup final and enjoyed a virtual monopoly of the Lancashire Cup throughout the early 1960s. Dagnall's undoubted ability to provide a stream of possession from the scrums impressed the international selectors and he played four times for Great Britain, twice against the visiting Kiwis in 1961 and against the French in 1964 and 1965.

During the 1965/66 season, Wigan's Bill Sayer came to Knowsley Road, giving the Saints an even bigger wealth of craft and experience in the hooking department. Although Sayer eventually became first choice, coach Joe Coan could afford to alternate both Sayer and Dagnall in the side throughout the campaign as the Saints stormed to a magnificent four-trophy success, including a Challenge Cup and Championship double.

Bob retired from the professional code in 1968 and joined the powerful St Helens Recs amateur outfit for a spell. 'Daggy' then turned to coaching with the St Helens Colts team, something that he found particularly rewarding. 'If you got so much out of the game like I did,' he recalled, 'then you get a lot of pleasure in putting something back. It was so gratifying to watch someone like Harry Pinner come through the ranks to full international level.' A member of the Saints' Past Players' Hall of Fame, Bob built up a successful joinery business with his close friend Johnny Fishwick, which they began in 1957 and he maintained a keen interest in events at Knowsley Road until his untimely death after a brave fight against cancer in 1999. He was one of the most popular Saints' players of his generation and is sadly missed by his legion of friends and former teammates.

Bob Doherty
Winger 1895-1903

Previous club: Kendal Hornets

St Helens debut: 7 September 1895 v. Rochdale Hornets

Final St Helens appearance: 31 January 1903 v. Swinton

Appearances: 224

Tries: 38

Goals: 0

Points: 114

Transferred to: Retired

Representative honours: Lancashire

Bob Doherty, or 'Bob Doc' as he was known was a rising star in his native Kendal with the famous Hornets club and decided he would head south to play in a better class of football. Like his former teammates Billy Cross and William Whiteley, he chose St Helens. The Saints' supporters soon took the Cumbrian winger to their hearts. Although slight, at 5ft 4ins and barely ten and a half stone, he was deceptively strong and elusive. His tackling for a small man was exceptional and he could bring down opponents forty or fifty pounds heavier than himself.

Doherty was a member of the Saints' team that won its first-ever honour in rugby football – the Lancashire County Rugby Challenge Cup Second Division trophy, which was presented to their Cumbrian captain Billy Cross. Doherty had a magnificent season, together with local-born winger Tom Sudlow on the other flank; they scored 50 tries between them – a fantastic achievement! Twelve months later in the new Northern Rugby Football Union competition, he had the distinction of scoring the club's first-ever try, at home to Rochdale Hornets, on Saturday 7 September 1895, when the pint-sized winger intercepted a pass on the visitors' 25, swerved out of one tackle and broke away from the next, rolling head-over-heels for a marvellous score in Saints' eventual 8-3 success.

Bob Doc appeared in the first-ever Challenge Cup final, when Saints took on Batley at

Headingley in 1897. They were seven points down at half-time, until the little Cumbrian set up a marvellous riposte. Batley captain Goodall tried to drop a goal but sliced his effort straight to Doherty, who fielded the ball and shrugged off attempted tackles from Davies and Fitzgerald. A dummy to the supporting Jacques, a quick turn and a lovely pass fizzed out to his centre Traynor, who flew down the wing to score the first try Batley had conceded in the competition. Saints lost 10-3 and drew Batley the following year in the first round. Once again Saints scored the only try as Batley went on to retain the trophy. The scorer – Bob Doc.

Doherty played in the inaugural South West Lancs and Border Towns Cup final at the turn of the century, when the Saints defeated Runcorn at Widnes 6-0 after extra time – another first for the popular Cumbrian. Bob's playing wages were 12 shillings for a win, 10 shillings for a draw and 8 shillings for a loss and he received a benefit of just under £20 for twelve years' service. He was elected a life member of the St Helens Club and worked for St Helens Cleansing Department for forty-three years, spending much of his leisure time at Peasley Cross Conservative Club and died in 1942 aged seventy-two – a real Saints' great.

Bernard Dwyer
Loose forward, hooker 1985-1995

Previous club: Hare and Hounds ARLFC

St Helens debut: 27 February 1985 v. Hull

Final St Helens appearance: 26 November 1995 v. Hull

Appearances: 199 + 33 subs

Tries: 39

Goals: 60

Drop-goals: 1

Points: 277

Transferred to: Bradford Bulls

Representative honours: None

Born in the rugby hotbed of Thatto Heath, a district that has produced the likes of Alex Murphy and Austin Rhodes – and with a father who shone at amateur level – it was inevitable that the oval ball would feature prominently in the life of Bernard Dwyer. Bernard was very much a 'double agent' in his early career, representing Merseyside and Lancashire rugby union at Under-16 level and gaining an England cap. One of his teammates was Shaun Edwards. He did, however, play rugby league with Saints' Under-17s and the Hare and Hounds amateurs, from where he signed professional forms on 20 April 1984.

Dubbed the 'Perpetual Motion Man', Bernard was not the biggest forward, at just 5ft 10ins and fourteen stone. Yet he was blessed with a phenomenal work rate, embracing relentless tackling, the ability to put in a telling pass and the knack of breaking through opposing defences from acting half-back which earned him a multitude of Man of the Match awards at Knowsley Road. Although his favourite position was loose forward, he played mostly in the back row or at hooker for the Saints – a position he gradually took over from Paul Groves in the early 1990s.

Making his debut at Hull as a substitute in the First Division Championship match against Hull at The Boulevard on 27 February 1985, Bernard gradually cemented a place in the first team squad with some all-action displays. He played in six major finals with the Saints during his career, winning just one, the 1993 Premiership final against Wigan. Bernard appeared in two Challenge Cup finals, only to be beaten on both occasions by Wigan. In 1989 the Cherry and Whites romped to a 27-0 success, but Bernard could have swung the game Saints' way in the 1991 clash, with a fantastic break from acting half-back in first half injury time, that nearly resulted in a vital try for winger Les Quirk.

Bernard (Barney) formed a superb double act with the great Kevin Ward (Fred), when the ex-Castleford front-rower came to Knowsley Road in 1990 and he took over goal-kicking duties for a spell, kicking twelve goals in a match against Trafford Borough in a Lancashire Cup tie in 1991. Yet just after his testimonial season, he was sensationally transferred to Bradford Bulls, together with Sonny Nickle and Paul Loughlin in exchange for star centre Paul Newlove. Indeed, Dwyer played against the Saints at Wembley in 1996 and 1997, but was a loser once again! After so much heartache, no-one begrudged him winning that elusive Challenge Cup winner's medal, when Bradford beat Leeds in 2000. Bernard coached the Academy team at Odsal for a spell before taking a job in the prison service. For sheer effort and commitment in the Saints' jersey, there was nobody better.

Alf Ellaby
Winger 1926-1934/1937-1939

Previous club: Rotherham AFC

St Helens debut: 27 March 1926 v. Keighley

Final St Helens appearance: 28 January 1939 v. Huddersfield

Appearances: 289

Tries: 280

Goals: 0

Points: 840

Transferred to: Wigan (First spell), Retired (Second spell)

Honours: Lancashire, England, Great Britain, RLXIII

Born in St Helens, on 24 November 1902 and one of eight children, Alfred Henry Ellaby was destined to become a rugby league immortal, who found fame on two continents between the Wars. Cast in the classical winger's mould at just over 6ft and weighing twelve stone, Ellaby had great pace and the ability to pick up even the most wayward pass from his centre. He was a try-scoring sensation at Knowsley Road, who could always be relied upon to add an extra couple of thousand to the crowd. Ellaby flew in for 280 touchdowns in 289 appearances for the Saints – figures exceeded only by Tom van Vollenhoven and Les Jones. Dubbed 'The Hat-trick King,' he notched 3 tries on 31 occasions for the Saints, and was the first player to score a half-century of tries in a season at Knowsley Road – with 55 in 40 matches in 1926/27. Alf toured Australia with both the 1928 and 1932 Great Britain squads and made thirteen Test appearances overall. Capped by Lancashire on nineteen occasions, he touched down seventeen times for the Red Rose county. Ellaby scored after just thirty seconds in the First Test against Australia at the Sydney Cricket Ground in 1932 and he captained his country in the first-ever international against France in Paris in 1934.

Alf's first love was soccer and he was a good enough centre half to sign as a professional for Rotherham United, until knee trouble was thought to have ended his career in his early twenties. The prognosis was rather premature, however, and on returning to St Helens he was practically bullied by Ted Smith, the Saints' sponge man, to join in with some training sessions at Knowsley Road. He found he had a natural aptitude for the game and with his knee problem cleared up, he made his first team debut against Keighley on 27 March 1926 and scored two tries. In his second home game against Bradford Northern, he scored his first hat-trick – and the tries just kept on coming. Alf's astonishing rise to prominence included county and international recognition in his first full season, together with a Lancashire Cup winner's medal in the defeat of local rivals Recs 10-2 at a packed Wilderspool ground in Warrington.

He was the man to kick-start the Saints' quest for major honours in the mid 1920s – a veritable 'crock in a million'! Alf developed an almost

ST. HELENS TOURISTS.

Recs.:- L. FAIRCLOUGH O. DOLAN A. ELLABY A. FILDES B. HALFPENNY F. BOWEN A. FRODSHAM

telepathic relationship with his centre and captain, George Lewis. Yet it didn't matter if George threw out a high or a wide pass, it would make no difference. He possessed such amazing flexibility, that he could stoop when on the run and pick up a ball from the ground without stopping. Alf was one of seven St Helens-based players – three from the Recs, four from the Saints – who were selected for the 1928 Great Britain tour. The tourists won the first two Tests against the Australians at Brisbane and Sydney, with Ellaby scoring vital tries in both of them. The 'Tin Hare' as the Aussies called him, scored no fewer than 20 tries on the tour, including 4 in 5 Test matches.

One of his biggest disappointments came after the defeat by unfancied Widnes at Wembley, when the Saints lost 10-3, especially after his two tries helped to see off those redoubtable cup fighters Wigan in the replayed semi-final at Mather Lane, Leigh. Alf won two Lancashire League medals with the Saints, yet ironically, his international status prevented him from playing in the 1932 Championship final, against Huddersfield at Wakefield, the club's first-ever victory. He was already en route to Australia, with teammate Albert Fildes.

Alf was a thoughtful, intelligent man and a true Corinthian, who detested foul play. He was always critical of some of the tactics in international

football, which he considered brutal and unnecessary. Skill and guile were always the best way – as he showed in the international between England and Wales at Wigan in 1928, when he did the unthinkable – scored a hat-trick against the great Jim Sullivan. His performance that day showed what a truly great performer he was, using change of pace to great effect and the ability to stop dead in his tracks to bamboozle the most famous fullback in the world.

In 1934 Alf Ellaby was transferred to deadly rivals Wigan for £800. The money spelt financial security for the Saints, who were close to bankruptcy at the time. 'The club was never the same after Alf went,' recalled George Lewis. 'The following Good Friday he scored a try against us – and he was positively apologetic about it. His heart was not really in the Wigan club.' Ellaby returned to the Saints for a couple of years before the war, but it wasn't quite the same.

Alf was, at various times, the landlord of the Veevers Arms and Ardwick Hotel in Blackpool, together with the George Hotel at Garforth, becoming a director of Castleford for a spell. A member of the Saints' Past Players' Hall of Fame, he lived in Garforth until his death at the age of ninety in 1993, when his ashes were scattered on the turf of his beloved Knowsley Road.

Leslie Fairclough
Stand-off 1917-1932

Previous club: YMCA

St Helens debut: 5 February 1921 v. Rochdale Hornets

Final St Helens appearance: 29 October 1932 v. Batley

Appearances: 355

Tries: 84

Goals: 3

Points: 258

Transferred to: Retired

Representative honours: Lancashire, England, Great Britain

Leslie Fairclough had signed for the Saints on Christmas Day 1917, when he was on leave from the Army, having enlisted some time previously as a drummer boy in the Fourth South Lancashire regiment. Earlier still, he had been a schoolboy star at Rivington Road School and it was his old headmaster – and Saints' chairman – Tom Phillips, who signed him on. Fairclough played his first match in the 'A' team on a wet day in 1919, alongside a scrum-half called Walter Groves, but it is hard to believe that the lad who was to become Saints' greatest home-grown stand-off was initially sent back to the Junior Leagues because he was deemed to be too small for professional rugby.

Yet Fairclough returned to Knowsley Road and the still frail-looking eighteen-year-old made his debut in the home match against Rochdale Hornets on 5 February 1921. Despite Saints' 10-0 demise, Fairclough more than caught the eye. Les had the toughest of baptisms, playing against the fearsome Rochdale half-back Ernie Jones. Reputations meant nothing to the Little Drummer Boy, however, and on this occasion Big Ernie found it extremely difficult to get to grips with his young opponent. Fairclough stood well away from the pack, took the ball on the run, put it to the centres and then came round for the return

pass, with all the finesse and composure of a veteran. He was later to resume his partnership with Walter Groves that became one of the most reliable – and durable – combinations in the League.

Leslie went on to play 355 matches for the Saints and although not a prolific try-scorer as such, was one of the most creative stand-off halves in the game. One of his best seasons was 1926/27, when he scored 17 tries from 37 appearances, including a vital touchdown against local rivals Recs at Warrington in the Lancashire Cup final. After fifteen minutes of an engrossing derby clash, Saints' centre Alf Frodsham caught the ball from some loose play and put in a tantalising grubber kick which caught the Recs' defence flat-footed. Les Fairclough, following up, picked up the ball cleverly on the bounce, beat second-rower Albert Fildes with a beautiful swerve and shot under the posts for a superb opportunist try. The Saints went on to lift the Lancashire Cup for the first time in their history by 10-2, after a further try by wing sensation Alf Ellaby, who was to benefit immensely from Fairclough's excellent service to his centres.

Fairclough was an integral member of the side described as the 'Team of all the Talents' that

ENGLAND'S N.U. TEST TEAM, OCT. 5th, 1929.
Mr. Hutchins   Burgess   Kinnear   Feetham   Middleton   Horton   Bowman   Mr. Lingard
                Dinsdale   Frodsham   F. Rees   Fairclough   Bentham   Thompson
                           B. Rees   Gwynne

won the Lancashire League title in 1930, but fell, disappointingly, at the last hurdle to Widnes in the Challenge Cup final at Wembley. Les was outstanding in both semi-finals against Wigan, however, keeping hopes alive in the 5-5 draw in the first match at Swinton. He gave a veritable masterclass of stand-off play in their 22-10 success in the replay at Mather Lane, Leigh, having a hand in all his team's four touchdowns. He beat three Wigan defenders with a seemingly effortless swerve and change of pace before setting up Saints' third three-pointer, which was finished off, inevitably, by his Great Britain teammate Alf Ellaby.

Leslie played a record twenty-one times for Lancashire, a distinction he holds with Bryn Evans of Swinton. His first appearance was against Yorkshire at Oldham on 8 December 1924 and he made his international debut for England in the 27-22 success over Wales just over twelve months later. His elusiveness and marvellous hands made him an automatic choice for the 1928 Australian tour, together with three of his teammates, Alf Ellaby (wing), Alf Frodsham (centre) and second-rower Ben Halfpenny. Despite certain reservations as to the relative strengths of the squad, Les Fairclough and Ellaby played a big part in defeating

the Australians and bringing home the Ashes. Both excelled on the hard grounds Down Under and scored crucial tries in the First Test at Brisbane, as Great Britain won by 15-12. Fairclough missed the Second Test through injury, but scored a brace in the Third Test in Sydney. Les captained Great Britain in the next Test against the Kangaroos at Hull on 5 October 1929, although the home side lost heavily. It was his last match against the Australians, yet he continued as the regular stand-off for both Lancashire and England in 1930/31.

It was unfortunate that a persistent knee injury denied Fairclough a League Championship medal in 1932, when he played a mere nine matches. After an abortive comeback in 1932/33, he called it a day after an outstanding career in domestic and international rugby. When he was offered the chance of a testimonial match, he insisted that the proceeds were shared with his old teammate Walter Groves – typical of his selfless nature. A publican, Leslie became a member of the Saints' committee after the Second World War, but unfortunately died from cancer in 1951 aged forty-nine – a sad loss indeed. He and Alf Ellaby are the most influential Saints' players in the era before the Second World War – renowned in both Britain and Australia.

David Fairleigh

Front-row forward 2001

Previous club: Newcastle Knights (Australia)

St Helens debut: 26 January 2001 v. Brisbane Broncos

Final St Helens appearance: 6 October 2001 v. Wigan Warriors

Appearances: 31 + 1 sub

Tries: 8

Goals: 0

Points: 32

Transferred to: Retired

Representative honours: None

It speaks volumes for the impact David Fairleigh made at Knowsley Road for him to be considered for a place in the club's list of all-time greats after just one campaign in the red and white jersey. He added extra power and mobility to an already formidable pack and finished his one and only season as a Saint as a member of the Super League dream team, picking up a World Club Championship and a Challenge Cup winner's medal on the way. His commitment was total and he seemed to play every match as though it was his last, making him a real cult figure with the fans.

Born in Gosford, NSW on 1 September 1970, David made his name with the famous North Sydney club as a second-rower. He played in four State of Origin series and was a member of the 1994 Kangaroo tourists to Great Britain, where he made fourteen appearances, including two Tests. The 1994 Rothman's Medal winner, he was signed from the Newcastle Knights club, together with his teammate Peter Sheils, on a one-year contract for the 2001 season.

In front of over 16,000 at Bolton's Reebok Stadium, David Fairleigh made an impressive debut for the club, with a display characterised by hard, straight running and seemingly impregnable defence as the Saints gradually ground down their opponents, Brisbane Broncos, in the second half for a marvellous 20-18 victory and the title of World Club Champions. He scored a superb try in the League match against Bradford Bulls at Valley

Parade and was prominent in the 22-8 Challenge Cup defeat of Wigan Warriors at Knowsley Road. In the pouring rain in the final against Bradford Bulls at Twickenham, Fairleigh produced another powerhouse display, especially in the second half, when the Bulls were chasing the game.

A statistical review of Fairleigh's season reveals why he was so effective. In 25 matches, he made 532 tackles and carried the ball up on 408 occasions, for a total of 3,344 metres. David also made 51 off-loads and 71 tackle busts – little wonder he was rated so highly by coach Ian Millward. Injuries prevented a repeat of the club's Grand Final success from 2000, however, as the team finished in fourth spot. Fairleigh himself severely damaged his shoulder against Leeds on 7 September, which eventually led to his retirement from the game, a great pity, as he had signed a twelve-month extension to his contract in July and looked forward to lining up with fellow Australian Darren Britt in the front row in 2002; but it was not to be. Yet he remains one of the most powerful and mobile front-rowers ever to play at Knowsley Road. On returning Down Under, he became an assistant coach at Newcastle Knights and has become a popular media figure.

Albert Fildes
Second-row forward 1930-1934

Previous club: St Helens Recreation

St Helens debut: 4 October 1930 v. Dewsbury

Final St Helens appearance: 1 September 1934 v. Widnes

Appearances: 129

Tries: 19

Goals: 0

Points: 57

Transferred to: Retired

Representative honours: Lancashire, England, Great Britain

Runcorn-born Albert Fildes was already a major star with local rivals St Helens Recreation with a formidable reputation in club and international football when the Saints signed him on 24 September 1930. Albert formed a legendary back three at the Recs, with Tommy Smith and loose forward Bill Mulvanney – a combination feared throughout the League. He played in three Lancashire Cup finals and a Championship final for the Recs and was one of seven players from the two St Helens clubs to be selected for the Australian tour in 1928.

Tremendously strong with supreme tackling ability, Fildes led a formidable Saints' pack that also included his fellow tourist Ben Halfpenny and a tall, aggressive second-rower by the name of Jack Arkwright. Aided and abetted by a pacy three-quarter line, with wingers Roy Hardgrave and Alf Ellaby sharing 77 tries between them, Albert enjoyed a particularly successful campaign in 1931/32 as the Saints clinched second place in the table and lifted the Lancashire League trophy. They won the last ten games of the campaign, with Fildes a tower of strength with his fantastic work rate and cover-tackling. He also showed his ability in the loose with nine tries during the season.

Albert and flying-winger Alf Ellaby missed the Championship semi-final against Leeds and the final itself against Huddersfield at Belle Vue, Wakefield – Saints' first-ever Championship success. They were on the boat to Australia, with Fildes joining Ellaby in the side for the crucial Third Test at Sydney on 16 July. Britain roared back from a 9-0 deficit to win 18-15 and retain the Ashes. Albert played 19 matches overall, scoring 6 tries and it was a whitewash in New Zealand, with Fildes playing in the First and last Tests, both in Auckland. In the Third, he scored a try as Great Britain won 20-18 on what was the final match of the tour. On their return to St Helens, both players were awarded a Championship winner's medal by the Knowsley Road club.

Albert scored a try in the Saints' 9-10 loss to a strong Warrington outfit in the Lancashire Cup final at Central Park in November 1932 and he was once again on the losing side in the Challenge Cup semi-final at the hands of the same opponents later in the campaign. The great team of the early thirties started to break up shortly after, largely a result of financial constraints and Albert retired early in the 1934/35 season after a marvellous career. He was a popular figure in St Helens' town centre as mine host of the White Hart Hotel in Church Street for many years. Saints' supporters wished Fildes had been signed a few years earlier, yet he was still highly regarded by all at the Knowsley Road club – a true great of the game between the wars.

Jim Flanagan

Winger, centre, stand-off 1908-1915

Previous club: Junior rugby league

St Helens debut: 5 September 1908 v. Oldham

Final St Helens appearance: 1 May 1915 v. Huddersfield

Appearances: 231

Tries: 125

Goals: 3

Points: 381

Transferred to: Killed in action

Representative honours: Lancashire

A local product, who played soccer in his youth, Jim Flanagan had all the attributes of a great winger. At 5ft 8ins in height and eleven and a half stone, he was quick, elusive and had excellent handling skills that would make him a fine centre later in his career. The young Flanagan made his debut in a 38-0 loss at home to Oldham at the start of the 1908/09 season, on the left wing, and rapidly became established as a first team regular. In 1909/10 the fair-haired flyer scored tries like they were going out of fashion, with 31 from 35 matches – a stunning statistic, putting him third in the League's try-scorers' list, the highest-ever placing for a St Helens player at the time. The team also reached the dizzy heights of tenth in the League table – a measure of the tremendous attacking power provided by the three-quarter line. Indeed, Flanagan's marvellous form continued in 1910/11, with 30 tries from 34 appearances and he formed a devastating partnership with Yorkshire-born centre Jimmy Greenwood that was feared throughout the League.

His scoring exploits earned him a county trial for Lancashire, where he caught the eye of the selectors with two stunning tries. His county debut came against Cumberland at Barrow in October 1909, on the left wing, one of six appearances in total for the Red Rose county over the next five years.

It was his biggest disappointment that international selection eluded him, although Jim did play against the visiting Australian tourists on two occasions, scoring a try in Saints' spectacular 9-0 victory over the Kangaroos in February 1909. He was truly devastating at club level, playing 151 matches on the wing (99 tries), 76 at centre (25 tries) and 4 as a stand off, scoring a try. Jim notched 4 tries on 3 occasions and five hat-tricks during his seven years as a Saint. His superb fitness also meant that he rarely missed a match in that time.

Honours with St Helens were relatively few and far between, including a couple of beaten Lancashire Cup semi-final appearances, although he took part in the Saints' famous Challenge Cup run in 1914/15 as centre to Tom Barton, when the team reached the final, only to be well beaten 37-3 by Huddersfield's 'Team of all the Talents'. It was to be his last match for the club. Like his former team-mates 'Jum' Turtill and Jimmy Greenwood, Sergeant Jim Flanagan paid the ultimate sacrifice while serving his country in the First World War, when he was killed by shrapnel on 14 May 1918 at just thirty-one years of age. Jim will always be remembered as one of the true greats of the pre-First World War era at Knowsley Road – a superb footballer, who served his club and county admirably.

Paul Forber
Front-row, second-row forward 1981-1993

Previous club: St Helens Colts

St Helens debut: 17 October 1982 v. Australia

Final St Helens appearance: 11 November 1992 v. Leigh

Appearances: 176 + 71 subs

Tries: 50

Goals: 7

Drop-goals: 1

Points: 215

Transferred to: Salford

Representative honours: Lancashire

If winner's medals were given out for dedication, courage and durability, Paul Forber would have them by the bucket-load. A local lad, he would have run through a brick wall for the sake of the team, if his own powerful running and astute ball distribution had failed to do the trick. Yet Paul had his fair share of injuries as a Saint, including the dire threat that after almost ten years at Knowsley Road he faced possible paralysis if he were to continue playing as a result of a serious shoulder injury, where the nerves had almost been shot away! Fortunately, he was able to resume where he left off – the same man who played in a cup-tie at Warrington less than ten days after a cartilage operation, scoring a brilliant try in the process.

Born in the famous Thatto Heath district of St Helens, Paul Forber had the perfect rugby league pedigree – his father, Ernie, had played with distinction for the old Liverpool City (later Huyton) club for many years. Paul played rugby union at Grange Park Secondary School, initially as a goal-kicking fly-half. Yet the fifteen-a-side code was not for him and he played with distinction for the St Helens Colts side, before turning professional on 29 April 1981. By this time Paul had filled out into a strong, forceful second-rower, with a huge appetite for work.

A real character, universally nicknamed 'Buffer' by teammates and fans, Paul soon had a testing introduction into the rigours of first team football, in a weakened Saints team for the match against the visiting Kangaroos in 1982. It was to be a real baptism of fire against the likes of Wayne Pearce, Les Boyd and company, as the Saints were swamped 32-0, but Forber showed great promise and was not fazed at all by the occasion.

Paul went on to play in seven major finals for the club – winning three, including two Challenge Cup finals (1987 and 1989), two Premiership finals (1985 and 1988), two Lancashire Cup finals (1991 and 1992) and a John Player final (1988). Indeed, he was unlucky not to be selected for the 1988 tour Down Under after showing his best form during the season. Paul was also used as a successful impact player by coach Alex Murphy, coming off the bench to add extra power to the pack when it was most needed. A county representative, he will always be remembered for scoring Saints' winning try in a fantastic 27-26 victory over a strong New Zealand side in 1989.

After a successful testimonial season, Paul joined Salford in November 1993 and became a crowd favourite at the Willows during the early Super League era. He coached Nutgrove amateurs and later made a brief comeback for Haydock, but his heart and soul remain forever entrenched at Knowsley Road.

Tom Foulkes
Full-back 1895-1906

Previous club: Ravenhead St Johns

St Helens debut: 7 September 1895 v. Rochdale Hornets

Final St Helens appearance: 30 April 1906 v. Salford

Appearances: 301

Tries: 3

Goals: 32

Points: 82

Transferred to: Retired

Representative honours: Lancashire

How times have changed. On 23 April 1904, promotion-chasing St Helens thrashed Lancaster 36-2 at Knowsley Road in the Second Division of the Northern Rugby Football League. The match had been set apart as the benefit of Tom Foulkes, the veteran full-back who was to retire at the end of the season after fifteen years' service to the club. Thatto Heath-born Foulkes began with St Helens in 1889/90, the last season at the old ground in Dentons Green, before the move to Knowsley Road. His previous experience of football was with his local Ravenhead St Johns club as a half-back. Saints signed him after watching him in a works medal competition.

Despite breaking both wrists in his first season, a start which would have ended many a player's career, he settled down to become one of the finest full-backs in the North of England, with a strong kicking game, coupled with resolute defence. County honours soon followed and he represented Lancashire on eleven occasions, ten under the rugby union. He was on the losing side just twice; both against Yorkshire.

For seven out of his fifteen seasons, from 1896/97, he was club captain. His first season as skipper was a memorable one as Saints reached the Challenge Cup final against Batley, only to lose 10-3 to the more powerful Yorkshire outfit. Although bitterly disappointed with the result, Tom was the first to congratulate the Batley players after the final whistle.

Tom's fearless, dashing style endeared him to Saints' supporters, and he repaid them with unswerving loyalty – despite offers from elsewhere. In the early part of his career in the so-called amateur days, he made a few appearances for the crack Oldham club. In the dressing room after one game he found a sovereign in each boot, together with an invitation to go for a slap-up meal in a posh Manchester hotel.

Such inducements proved most attractive to young Foulkes, especially when they offered him a job to go with a place in their team. He decided he would throw in his lot with the Roughyeds, and went to Shaw Street station with his luggage to catch the train for Oldham. Although he was sorely tempted, the money was not everything. The prospect of leaving his close pals Kitty Briers and Ned Ashcroft did not appeal to him that much. He promptly returned home, unpacked his bags and asked for his job back at Cannington-Shaws bottleworks, where he was an apprentice sorter. That was Tom Foulkes, a St Helens man through and through! Tom also served on the Saints' committee for many years and his grandson, Bill, found fame as a centre half with both Manchester United and England as a member of the Busby Babes. A life member of the St Helens club, Tom died in 1953 aged eighty-one.

Ray French
Second-row forward 1961-1967

Previous club: St Helens RUFC

St Helens debut: 30 August 1961 v. Wakefield Trinity

Final St Helens appearance: 28 August 1967 v. Wakefield Trinity

Appearances: 201 + 3 subs

Tries: 10

Goals: 0

Points: 30

Transferred to: Widnes

Representative honours: Lancashire, Rugby League XIII

A local lad, educated at the famous Cowley Boys Grammar School, Ray signed for Saints from St Helens RUFC in the summer of 1961. He was already an England rugby union international, brought in to refresh the pack that had steered Saints to the Lancashire Cup and Challenge Cup the previous season. No stranger to the rigours of rugby league, he became an uncompromising second-rower and a belligerent tackler. Little did he realise that after the end of his playing career, he would take up the mantle of BBC television commentator, from the great Eddie Waring.

The Saints went on to retain the Lancashire Cup in the 1961/62 campaign, with French very much a workhorse in the pack, with his ability to drive the ball up *ad infinitum* and tackle everything that moved. He was not a try-scoring forward, as such, but one try will long be remembered, in the 10-7 victory over Swinton in the 1964 Western Division final, when he plunged over the line after taking a short pass from John Tembey. Ray won a second Lancashire Cup winner's medal in 1963, against Leigh, and he was to make history at the start of the 1964/65 campaign, when he entered the field as Saints' first-ever substitute, in the away match at

Hilton Park, Leigh. The team were League leaders and Lancashire League winners that year, a feat they were to replicate, and more besides, in 1965/66, as pack leader Ray turned in barn-storming displays in the Challenge Cup final against Wigan, and the Championship final in the 35-12 rout of Halifax.

A Lancashire county representative with Saints, Ray stepped into the breach as captain, following Alex Murphy's dispute with the club in the following season. The introduction of the four-tackle rule reduced the effectiveness of the Saints' pack in wearing down the opposition, but French led the Saints to a third successive Lancashire League Championship and the team were runners-up in the Championship final against Wakefield Trinity after a replay. Yet there was no sentiment in rugby league in those days. At the start of 1967/68, Ray was transferred to Widnes – he was painting the front of his house when he heard that he was being part-exchanged for Frank Myler, the Widnes and Great Britain stand-off half.

Later in his career, he became more of a play-maker and ball distributor, gaining full international honours at Widnes – and a place in the 1968 World Cup squad Down Under. He remains a leading rugby league pundit and a tireless worker for the game – a prolific author and match commentator for both radio and television. Ray is still a familiar face around Knowsley Road where he is currently the chairman of the Past Players' Association and a member of the Association's Hall of Fame.

Previous club: Pilkington Recreation RUFC (Doncaster)

St Helens debut: 26 December 1922 v. Wigan

Final St Helens appearance: 26 October 1929 v. Castleford

Appearances: 210

Tries: 88

Goals: 3

Points: 270

Transferred to: St Helens Recreation (First spell), Retired (Second spell)

Representative honours: Lancashire, England, Great Britain

A member of a sporting family from Pigot Street in St Helens, Alf Frodsham was on Saints' books as an amateur from an early age but allowed to drift. He was playing rugby union at Doncaster, for the Pilkington Works' team, and attracted the attention of Huddersfield and Halifax. On hearing this, Alf was invited by the St Helens' board to play in the Boxing Day clash at home to Wigan in 1922 and signed on professional forms afterwards. He gradually cemented a regular place in the first team, essentially as a centre, although he could play anywhere in the back line with equal effectiveness.

Alf wore the No.3 jersey as a member of the famous St Helens team that brought the Lancashire Cup home to Knowsley Road for the first time in the club's history, against Recs on 20 November 1926. Fast and direct, Frodsham scored 22 tries during the campaign and came to the notice of the county selectors. Playing on the right wing (club-mate Alf Ellaby was on the other flank), he scored on his debut for Lancashire in a stunning 28-3 victory over New Zealand at Leigh. Before the end of the season, he was left centre in the England team that defeated Wales 11-8 at the Cliff, Broughton.

Overall, Alf made five appearances for Lancashire in the County Championship and won them all, with a further match against Australia, at Warrington in 1929. He gave a stunning performance during the 1928 tour trial at Headingley, when he scored three superb tries for the Whites against the Reds, which assured him of a place in the squad to visit Australia and New Zealand – one of four Saints' players to make the trip (Alf Ellaby, Les Fairclough and Ben Halfpenny were the others). Alf made 17 appearances on tour, scoring 15 tries. He played in the Second and Third Tests in New Zealand, which Great Britain won to clinch the rubber.

He was on the verge of further glory with the Saints when he was transferred to local rivals Recs for £450, in February 1929 – a result of his dissatisfaction at not being guaranteed a benefit at the end of his career. The emergence of young centre Bill Mercer and the signing of New Zealand winger Roy Hardgrave also made competition for places very intense. Ironically, Alf went on to pick up his second Lancashire Cup winner's medal when the Recs beat Wigan 18-3 at Station Road. Alf returned to Knowsley Road briefly as a player in 1937 and took over as first team coach for a spell just after the War. Brother Harry followed him into the Saints' team as a scrum-half and another brother, Eric, found fame as a full-back with Warrington. A sporting family indeed.

Peter Glynn
Stand-off 1974-1983

Previous club: Widnes Junior RL

St Helens debut: 31 August 1975 v. Oldham

Final St Helens appearance: 27 March 1983 v. Carlisle

Appearances: 244 + 14 subs

Tries: 118

Goals: 86

Drop-goals: 5

Points: 531

Transferred to: Salford

Representative honours: Lancashire, England

A product of Widnes amateur rugby, Peter Glynn could play with equal effectiveness at half-back, wing, centre or full-back. Speedy and elusive, he had superb hands, was a great reader of a game and, above all, he had brilliant anticipation to sniff out those vital tries when occasions demanded it. He signed for the Saints in the summer of 1974 and made a try-scoring debut at stand-off in the victory over Oldham on 31 August 1975.

By the end of his first season, he became known as 'Supersub' with his efforts in the 1976 Challenge Cup final, against his home-town club. After replacing veteran stand-off Billy Benyon at half-time, Peter scored a vital try that gave the Saints a crucial 12-5 advantage in the searing heat. Geoff Pimblett and Tony Karalius engineered the four-pointer, following an incredible eighty-yard run from winger Les Jones. With two minutes to go, as Saints pounded the Widnes line, Peter kicked over, re-gathered and slammed the ball down for his second try, despite the efforts of Dennis O'Neill, setting the seal on a magnificent victory for St Helens' 'Dad's Army' side. Two weeks later, Peter appeared at centre in the Premiership final against a strong Salford outfit at Swinton. Saints over-ran their opponents in the last

quarter, but it was all started by Peter Glynn, who started and finished a move which included Roy Mathias and George Nicholls. This score effectively broke the Salford resistance and Saints romped in for two more tries to win by 15-2.

Peter became a regular at stand-off, or centre, at Knowsley Road and he played a dominant role in the 1977 Premiership final defeat of Warrington, with his excellent ball skills. Indeed, Peter was reaching his peak as a footballer, just at a time when the St Helens club itself was slipping into a period of relative decline. He topped the appearances chart in the 1977/78 campaign, scoring five brilliant tries in the 52-14 victory over Hull, where his brilliant support play and clinical finishing were shown to great effect. Peter played at left centre in the 1978 Challenge Cup final against Leeds, who lifted the trophy after a thrilling second-half fight-back and he finished the campaign with no fewer than 28 touchdowns.

Peter's form was good enough to warrant inclusion in the 1979 Australian tour party, although he did not play in any of the Tests. He did win two England caps and represented Lancashire six times during his Saints' career. He continued to inspire his colleagues over the next few years, before his transfer to Salford at the end of the 1982/83 season. He enjoyed prodigious success at the start of his career and helped guide the Saints through a difficult period of transition, in the late seventies and early eighties.

Peter Gorley
Second-row forward 1979-1986

Previous club: Workington

St Helens debut: 9 October 1979 v. Rochdale Hornets

Final St Helens appearance: 2 February 1986 v. Featherstone Rovers

Appearances: 225 + 9 subs

Tries: 46

Goals: 0

Points: 150

Transferred to: Whitehaven

Representative honours: Cumberland, England, Great Britain

In the mould of other great forward signings from Cumbria, like John Tembey and Dick Huddart, Peter Gorley had a granite-like hardness. At 6ft 2ins and over fifteen stone – and seemingly all knees and elbows – he was extremely mobile for his size and was such a difficult player to put down in the tackle. Born on 10 July 1951 at Maryport, Peter appeared for Workington Town with distinction on 124 occasions, scoring 13 tries. His elder brother Les, cast in the same tough mould, packed down in the second row with him and later went on to further glory with the powerful Widnes team of the 1980s. Peter was a late arrival into the professional game, however, having played with his local Broughton team until the age of twenty-two.

Peter made his Workington debut in November 1975 and went from strength to strength. He appeared in three Lancashire Cup finals, winning one, and spent three of his four seasons in the First Division. He had played three times for Cumbria by the time he joined St Helens, in a £22,000 deal in October 1979. The Saints were in the throes of rebuilding when Peter came to Knowsley Road and, despite becoming a Great Britain international during his first few seasons with his new club, the team struggled to maintain a place in the top eight.

The 1984/85 campaign saw the Saints at last make a concerted challenge for honours, with Australian centre Mal Meninga an essential catalyst. Peter was a huge influence, having graduated to the front row, as the team won the Lancashire Cup final against Wigan at Central Park. Although pipped by Hull KR for the First Division title (their highest position since 1977), the Saints gained ample consolation with a stunning 36-16 Premiership final victory over those same opponents at Elland Road. Once again, Gorley was a cornerstone of the Saints' pack, with his unbridled commitment and work rate. Peter missed just one match during the campaign, playing over forty times, and formed one of the hardest-working front rows with teammate Tony Burke.

Despite the prospect of continuing the regular 250-mile round journey for training and matches in St Helens and beyond, thirty-four-year-old Peter played twenty-three matches in what was his final season at Knowsley Road in 1985/86, although a disagreement with coach Alex Murphy hastened his departure. He had been a real tower of strength at St Helens with his work rate and uncanny ability to offload the ball under pressure to supporting players with extra pace, such as scrum-half Neil Holding. A quiet man off the field, Peter was one of the most respected forwards of his generation – a real professional – and will always be remembered as a true Saints' great.

Bobbie Goulding
Scrum-half 1994-1998

Previous club: Widnes

St Helens debut: 21 August 1994 *v.* Doncaster

Final St Helens appearance: 26 July 1998 *v.* Wigan Warriors

Appearances: 115 + 2 subs

Tries: 25

Goals: 548

Drop-goals: 13

Points: 1,209

Transferred to: Huddersfield Giants

Representative honours: England, Great Britain

Bobbie Goulding had a reputation as a 'stormy petrel' when the Saints signed him from Widnes on 27 July 1994. Although still in his early twenties, he was an experienced player at club and international level. Born in Widnes, he joined Wigan from the local St Marie's amateur club, winning two Challenge Cups. He became the youngest-ever British Lion when selected for the 1990 tour to New Zealand, playing in all three Tests against the Kiwis, with Britain winning the rubber 2-1. A controversial character, who never took a backward step on the field, he later joined Leeds and Widnes before Saints swooped for a reputed £135,000 fee to land him on a three-year contract. An early publicity photograph showed Bobbie in Saints' blue and white centenary kit, complete with a cheeky grin and air-brushed halo.

Goulding had a superb season in 1994/95, making thirty-six appearances and although the Saints lost out to rivals Wigan in the 1996 Regal Trophy final at Huddersfield, there was much reason for optimism in the performance. Skipper Goulding led his young side into the new summer Super League with great confidence and maturity. He was chief playmaker,

with an excellent kicking game. His lateral running and drop-off passes brought star centre Paul Newlove a large percentage of his 36 tries during a campaign in which Goulding was the League's leading goal-kicker (162) and points scorer (348).

Yet his greatest moment was at Wembley Stadium, in the 1996 Challenge Cup final against Bradford Bulls, when the Saints found themselves 26-12 down after fifty-three minutes. Goulding unleashed three consecutive 'bombs' that realised three tries, from Cunningham, Booth and Pickavance. His improvisation completely turned the game on its head and St Helens eventually snatched the trophy by 40-32 in what has become one of the classic finals – the club's first Wembley success for twenty years.

In 1997, the Saints faced the same opponents again, defeating their Yorkshire rivals this time around with the emphasis on grubber-kicks. After Saints' 32-22 success, including six goals from Goulding, he allowed vice captain Chris Joynt to go up for the trophy. Bobbie had missed most of the earlier rounds through suspension.

It was a somewhat turbulent end to 1997 for St Helens, with an injury crisis badly affecting their World Club Championship campaign. Bobbie would never recapture the fantastic football he played in his first two years with the club and a parting of the ways became inevitable in August 1998, when he joined the Huddersfield Giants. It was a sad end to his Knowsley Road career, considering his supreme achievements in the 1996 season, when he guided his young Saints' team out of the trophy wilderness to the League and Cup double – definitely a case of being in the right place at the right time.

Centre 1946-1960

Previous club: *Rivington Road School*

St Helens debut: 10 April 1946 *v. Salford*

Final St Helens appearance: 5 December 1959 *v. Workington*

Appearances: 487

Tries: 188

Goals: 14

Points: 592

Transferred to: Wigan

Honours: Lancashire, England, Great Britain

was rarely sent off in his career. Perhaps the best man to explain his rather unique tackling style was his former wing partner Steve Llewellyn:

> His favourite technique was to come out near me so that he would be coming in to his opposing centre on the blind side, as it were. Then he would jump and, I think the best way to describe it, use his arms like a bow. Very often it was his chest that hit the man and his arms flailed round his opponent, and down they would go together. Sometimes the opposing centre didn't get up, but Duggie always seemed to get up.

A local lad, born on 7 June 1927, Duggie began his rugby career as an ATC cadet at Rivington Road school, under the command of future Saints' chairman Harry Cook. He signed for St Helens on 4 February 1946, for just £30. Duggie first appeared in a number of positions, including wing and stand-off, but he eventually settled down at centre and went on to representative honours. When Duggie began at Knowsley Road, the club was one of the poorer relations in the League. When he left fourteen years later, they had won the Lancashire Cup, Challenge Cup and had been League Champions twice – enough said.

Duggie was one of the best centres around, who could time a pass to perfection. He used to do an outside swerve, draw the opposing winger in, and slip the ball to his wing man at the last moment. Called 'Mr Muscles' by coach Jim Sullivan, Greenall tipped the scales at barely eleven and a half stone and was 5ft 9ins tall, yet he is best remembered for his amazing tackling. Despite his reputation as a bit of a tough customer, it was significant that Greenall

Greenall played in all three Tests against the Kiwis in 1951 and skippered the Saints in the 1952/53 campaign, when the club joined the rugby league elite. Sully's Boys won the Lancashire League title, were runners-up in the Lancashire Cup final and Challenge Cup and went on to lift the Championship after a fabulous victory over Halifax at Maine Road, Manchester. Duggie impersonated Al Jolson as a party piece and his rendition of 'Mammy' was always a great favourite. When the 1952 Kangaroos came to Knowsley Road, the Popular Side kept on shouting for their hero to 'give 'em Mammy' as the Saints gave them

the runaround. The Kangaroos refused to believe that such a lightweight footballer could cause such devastation, and claimed that 'Mammy' was the nickname for a secret plaster cast hidden under Duggie's sleeve. It was merely elastoplast, of course. These claims were taken seriously by the Australian press, especially when Greenall arrived Down Under with the 1954 Great Britain team. Fearing that his selection for the Test matches could possibly sour Anglo-Australian relations on a par with cricket's infamous Bodyline tour of 1930, government officials urged the tour management not to select him. Eventually, Ernie Ashcroft (Wigan) and Phil Jackson (Barrow) were selected to play in the centres in all three Tests. Although casualties on both sides were kept to a minimum, Britain went on to lose the Ashes by two matches to one.

Duggie played six times for England, three for Lancashire and was awarded a benefit match against Halifax in 1952 at the tender age of twenty-five. Greenall captained the team in the 1953 Lancashire Cup final success over Wigan and was a member of the side that brought the Challenge Cup back to St Helens for the first time, after defeating Halifax 13-2 in 1956. He went on to play in three more Lancashire Cup finals (runners-up on each occasion) and was a member of the team that lifted the Championship in

1959 after one of the greatest-ever finals, the 44-22 victory over Hunslet at Odsal Stadium. On the wing that day was the quicksilver South African Tom van Vollenhoven, who scored a fantastic hat-trick and owed much of his early success to the guile and experience of Duggie Greenall as his centre.

By January 1960, the man who made 487 appearances for St Helens decided he needed a new challenge and signed for Wigan. Before he left, the Saints' board presented him with an inscribed gold watch in recognition of his fourteen years' service to the club. After a disappointing twelve months at Central Park, however, Duggie moved to Bradford Northern for a spell before retiring to concentrate on his public house business in St Helens. He had become known as one of rugby league's most injured men, with an almost endless list of broken bones. 'I may have collected a few clouts in my time, but by God I dished out a few as well,' he recalled with typical relish.

He remained a prominent member of the Saints' Past Players' Association and is a member of their Hall of Fame. Duggie was in fine form during an interview for Sky Sports in 2005 and regaled everyone with the inevitable strains of his theme tune – Mammy. He remained a true character and a genuine rugby league legend.

Walter Groves

Scrum-half, loose forward 1915-1933

Previous club: Local juniors

St Helens debut: 18 September 1920 v. Warrington

Final St Helens appearance: 4 April 1933 v. Halifax

Appearances: 342

Tries: 49

Goals: 1

Points: 149

Transferred to: Retired

Representative honours: None

Every club needs a footballer like Walter Groves, a solid, reliable servant, with a real 'never-say-die' spirit. Although nicknamed 'Plodder,' he was no slouch and at his best he was quite devastating. He was more than capable of running rings round the famous international scrum-half Bryn Evans, during a brilliant 27-0 defeat of Swinton in 1927. A schoolboy star, Groves signed for the Saints in 1915, although he was in the Army for the next two years and made his 'A' team debut on demob, against local rivals St Helens Recs. Walter originally began as a centre, but was moved to scrum-half as a result of injury. Promotion came slowly and he made his first team debut against Warrington on 18 September 1920 at Knowsley Road when he scored his first try for the club.

Although he started to develop a partnership with another local star, Leslie Fairclough, Walter found that there were many obstacles to overcome before he made the No.7 jersey his own. Other scrum-halves came and went. He made occasional appearances in the first team, mostly in the three-quarters, but he kept going and never really lost heart, although he was once transfer listed at £250. The club saw sense and made peace again. It was a masterstroke, as Groves had no rivals from 1926 to 1930 at the base of the scrum, with his partner Leslie Fairclough developing into a world-class stand-off half.

Walter really enjoyed the derby clashes with the Recs and he played in the club's Lancashire Cup final success in 1926 against those same opponents

at Wilderspool, where he picked up his first winner's medal in the Saints' fantastic 10-2 success. Walter later suffered a serious facial injury when he fell forcibly on an icy pitch against Wigan at Knowsley Road, but fought back to fitness with his usual determination.

The Saints' 'Team of all the Talents' topped the League table in the 1929/30 campaign and reached Wembley, only to lose to unfancied Widnes. Yet in the semi-final replay against mighty Wigan, at Mather Lane, Leigh, it was Groves and his partner Fairclough who totally eclipsed their opposite numbers, Binks and Abrams, to guide St Helens to a memorable 22-10 success.

Back went Walter to the 'A' team, only to transform himself into a redoubtable loose forward and return to first team action where he belonged. A one-club man throughout his career, he helped the Saints to their first-ever Championship success, after a closely fought 9-5 victory over Huddersfield, alas without the injured Leslie Fairclough. Indeed, Walter was held in such high regard by Fairclough that when the club offered Leslie a benefit match against Warrington, in the 1930/31 season, he insisted that it should be a joint venture with his teammate Walter Groves – a fine gesture indeed.

Roy Haggerty

Centre, second-row forward 1978-1991

Previous club: St Helens Colts

St Helens debut: 30 October 1979 v. Widnes

Final St Helens appearance: 7 April 1991 v. Wakefield

Appearances: 320 + 43 subs

Tries: 115

Goals: 0

Drop-goals: 20

Points: 443

Transferred to: Barrow

Representative honours: Lancashire, Great Britain

The 1985/86 season was undoubtedly a mixed one for the Saints. Although no trophy ended up on the Knowsley Road sideboard, the team embarked upon an exciting run of fourteen wins from early February to the end of April, punctuated only by defeat at the hands of Wigan in the second round of the Challenge Cup. A tremendous influence during this remarkable sequence was Roy Haggerty, a likeable Thatto Heath lad who became a cult figure with the Popular Side fans. He even went on to finish top of the try-scoring chart with 21 tries – a fine feat indeed for a second-row forward in competition with such three-quarters as Barry Ledger at Knowsley Road.

A former pupil at Grange Park School, Roy Haggerty signed for the Saints in November 1978 and made his first team debut almost twelve months later on 30 October 1979 against Widnes, in a John Player Cup second round tie at Naughton Park. By 1981/82 Roy had established himself as a first team regular and his forceful runs in the centre brought him a respectable tally of twelve tries. There was no doubt at all that this youngster had a heart as big as the stand.

Perhaps the biggest challenge to Roy's first-team place came not from the critics but from the signing of Australian centre superstar Mal Meninga in 1984/85. Coach Billy Benyon had the answer, by switching him permanently to the second row. The change in Haggerty's form was immediate and Roy silenced the doubters with many fine displays, using his stuttering running style and great sidestep to deadly effect. Roy scored in the Lancashire Cup final against Wigan, thundering on to a Meninga pass to help Saints capture their first trophy in seven years. The Saints went on to capture the Premiership title in 1985, with Roy prominent in the final against Hull KR at Elland Road.

Roy had developed an excellent rapport with the crowd. A Lancashire county representative, he went on to win two caps for Great Britain in 1987, against the French. At club level, he played in two Wembley finals (1987 and 1989) and a Premiership final (1988) for the Saints, only to come out with a loser's medal on all three occasions. Yet there were further highlights for Roy, when he helped Saints to victory in the 1988 John Player Trophy final against Leeds at Central Park. His form was so good that he was selected for the Australian Tour at the end of the campaign – a superb achievement.

Roy played his last match as a Saint on 7 April 1991 at Wakefield and went on to play for Barrow and later Huddersfield. He was a local hero in St Helens, however; a natural footballer who rarely missed a game for his home-town club in his twelve-year career at Knowsley Road.

Ben Halfpenny

Second-row forward 1927-1934

Previous club: Widnes

St Helens debut: 10 September 1927 v. Swinton

Final St Helens appearance: 10 November 1934 v. Broughton Rangers

Appearances: 196

Tries: 59

Goals: 0

Points: 177

Transferred to: Warrington

Representative honours: England, Great Britain Tour

Born in Widnes in 1904, Ben Halfpenny was ahead of his time. He was essentially a running second-row forward, long before this became a specialist position for the likes of Dick Huddart in the late 1950s. Saints signed him from his hometown club for £250 on 18 April 1927 and he went on to become a huge favourite at Knowsley Road. Ben gained a reputation as a prolific try-scorer notching 16 tries in 31 appearances by the end of his first full season. He played in England's 20-12 victory against Wales on 11 January 1928 at Wigan, scoring a try and his form was such that he was later selected for the tour of Australia and New Zealand, one of seven St Helens-based players chosen to make the trip (Ben Halfpenny, Les Fairclough, Alf Frodsham and Alf Ellaby of the Saints; Oliver Dolan, Frank Bowen and Albert Fildes from local rivals the Recs).

According to the *St Helens Newspaper and Advertiser,* the likeable Halfpenny was described at the time as: '…a man of many parts. He is on the laboratory staff at Widnes United Alkali Works, plays the big bass fiddle, dances extremely well, weighs over thirteen stones and can do one hundred yards from scratch well under eleven seconds and is proud of the fact that he was born in Widnes – so he is indeed a very remarkable fellow.'

Alas, Ben did not figure in any of the Test matches, Down Under, playing in 10 games and scoring 8 tries, the second row spots being taken almost exclusively by Bob Sloman of Oldham and Frank Bowen of the Recs. Indeed, an injury from the tour restricted him to just eleven matches during 1928/29, but Ben was back to his best the following season, with 17 tries from 44 appearances, as the Saints clinched the Lancashire League title. He even played on the wing in place of the injured Alf Ellaby against the visiting Australians on 16 November 1929 and scored two brilliant touchdowns. Yet the campaign was to end in disappointment, with a fixture backlog of thirteen matches in thirty-five days taking its toll. Both the Challenge Cup final (v. Widnes) and Championship semi-final (v. Leeds) were lost, although Ben did add a Lancashire League winner's medal to his collection.

Halfpenny made thirty-one appearances in 1931/32, gaining his second Lancashire League winner's medal, and helped the Saints to win their first-ever Championship final, against Huddersfield at Belle Vue, Wakefield. Ben played thirty-five matches in the following season including fifteen outings in the front row, but his career at Knowsley Road was drawing to a close and he was transferred to Warrington in November 1934, as the St Helens club was forced to sell off its stars from the start of the decade as a result of a deepening financial crisis.

Roy Hardgrave
Winger 1929-1934

Previous club: New Zealand RL

St Helens debut: 31 August 1929 v. Widnes

Final St Helens appearance: 14 April 1934 v. London Highfield

Appearances: 212

Tries: 173

Goals: 0

Points: 519

Transferred to: York

Representative honours: Other Nationalities

New Zealander Roy 'Shaver' Hardgrave had played in the final Test at Christchurch against the 1928 tourists, which Great Britain won 6-5. Some months later, he wrote to his former adversary Alf Ellaby, expressing a desire to play in England. The astute Saints' legend immediately contacted the committee with regard to bringing him to St Helens. Shortly afterwards, at an emergency meeting, it was resolved to sign Hardgrave and, several days later, fellow international forwards Lou Hutt and Trevor Hall, when it became known that they were available.

At 5ft 7ins and nearly eleven stone, Hardgrave had great pace and a fantastic skipping sidestep that baffled opposing defenders. At twenty-two years of age, the 'Newton Flyer' soon settled down in St Helens and became a try-scoring phenomenon, flying in for 33 in 47 appearances in his first season, as the Saints reached top spot in the League table and clinched the Lancashire League title. Mighty Wigan were also defeated in a famous replay in the semi-final of the Challenge Cup at Mather Lane, Leigh. It was to be a disappointing climax to the season for the 'Three Hs,' however, as the 'Team of all the Talents' were defeated in controversial circumstances in the top four clash with Leeds, at Knowsley Road, despite a fine try from Hardgrave,

and at Wembley against Widnes, in one of the greatest-ever upsets in the competition's history.

Despite these set-backs, the Saints' wingers were on fire in 1930/31, with Ellaby scoring 43 to Hardgraves' 32. The following season Roy scored 44 tries to Ellaby's 33 as the Saints clinched second place in the table and lifted the Lancashire League trophy once more. They won the last ten League games in succession and the little Kiwi equalled Ellaby's feat of 1926/27 of scoring tries in nine successive club games in March and April 1932. He ended with 44 tries from 42 appearances – an astonishing statistic. The Saints went on to win their first-ever Championship, with a 9-5 success over Huddersfield at Wakefield, on 7 May 1932, ironically without Alf Ellaby, who was already on the boat, having been selected for the Australian tour.

Roy's fellow New Zealanders, Hutt and Hall, left St Helens at the end of the 1930/31 campaign. He remained a Saint, however, and played in the 1932 Lancashire Cup final defeat by Warrington. Roy continued to score freely, before returning to New Zealand at the end of the 1933/34 campaign. He later came back to play for York for a spell, yet his unbelievable scoring feats of almost a try per match – on a par with the great Tom van Vollenhoven in that respect – will always hold a special place for him in the history of St Helens Rugby League Club.

Jeff Heaton

Scrum-half 1960-63/1969-76

Previous club: Local juniors

St Helens debut: 30 August 1962 *v.* Liverpool City

Final St Helens appearance: 22 May 1976 *v.* Salford

Appearances: 279 + 12 subs

Tries: 68

Goals: 6

Drop-goals: 1

Points: 217

Transferred to: Liverpool City (First spell) Rochdale Hornets (Second spell)

Representative honours: None

During the 1970s, Saints' Jeff Heaton established himself as the best uncapped scrum-half in British rugby league. A local lad who came through the ranks at Knowsley Road, his story of success, second time around, is unique:

I signed for Saints in October 1960 and made my first team debut at the end of 1961/62 in a friendly against SHAPE Indians, a team of American Servicemen based in France. Alex Murphy returned from Australia in 1962 with a bad shoulder injury and I got in at the start of the new season, as did Bill Benyon, and we went on to beat Swinton 7-4 in the Lancashire Cup final. We were only kids – seventeen years of age! Well, Murphy came back – he was the world's number one scrum-half – and that was the end for me. I decided to accept Liverpool City's offer. I really enjoyed my football there and we played top class opposition every other week, which kept your game up to par. In September 1969, Basil Lowe asked me if I would like to return to Knowsley Road. I certainly had nothing to lose. The fee was £750… it was a great time for me to return – we were rarely out of the race for honours.

A great reader of the game, with excellent distribution, Heaton drove his forwards to magnificent back-to-back victories in the 1970 and 1971 Championship finals against Leeds and Wigan, the former with Frank Myler at stand-off. The 1971/72 campaign was to see Heaton at the peak of his powers – forming a dynamic half-back partnership with Ken Kelly in the Challenge

Cup final against Leeds and making an astonishing fifty-two appearances during the campaign; a measure of his great durability and consistency.

Jeff was first-choice scrum-half during the First Division Championship-winning season in 1974/75 and was to crown a magnificent career at Knowsley Road with his contributions in the 'treble' season that followed. The Saints beat Dewsbury in the Floodlit Trophy and reached the Challenge Cup final, courtesy of Heaton's crucial touchdown in the semi-final against Keighley. In the searing heat of Wembley, it was another crucial Heaton try, from a runaround move with Tony Karalius, which helped put the Saints on the glory trail, with just twelve minutes to go. Two weeks later, he added a Premiership final winner's medal to his impressive collection, after Salford were defeated 15-2. It was Jeff's last match as a Saint. Despite rumours of retirement, he went on to Rochdale for a further couple of years, to help his friend Kel Coslett, who had moved to the Recreation Grounds as player-coach. Jeff, who also helped to coach the Colts at Knowsley Road, is undoubtedly a Saints' great, inducted into the Saints' Past Players' Hall of Fame in 2004.

Neil Holding
Scrum-half 1977-1990

Previous club: Local juniors

St Helens debut: 23 January 1977 v. Swinton

Final St Helens appearance: 1 April 1990 v. Leeds

Appearances: 318 + 25 subs

Tries: 145

Goals: 84

Drop-goals: 44

Points: 739

Transferred to: Oldham

Representative honours: Lancashire, England, Great Britain

It was always difficult for the young Neil Holding when he was compared to the legendary Alex Murphy early in his career, yet he blossomed into a great player in his own right. The former junior starlet signed for his home-town club on 25 August 1977 and made his first team debut at Swinton as a seventeen-year-old two months later in a 28-11 victory, with Bill Francis as his stand-off. The ex-Rivington Road pupil was blessed with lightening pace and he would get himself in a position to accept offloads from his forwards, such as Peter Gorley, and streak away to the whitewash. He was also a master of the 'chip and chase'.

Neil played in the 1978 Floodlit Trophy final, won by Widnes and in the 1982 Lancashire Cup demise against Warrington. Although he still searched for that elusive winner's medal it was his head-down 'jackrabbit' running at pace that earned him Great Britain Under-24 recognition in the early 1980s, with three appearances against the French and one against New Zealand.

After a successful campaign in 1983/84, Neil, together with skipper Harry Pinner, was selected for the Australian tour and he played in all three

Tests against Australia, despite a nagging knee injury. The following year was Neil's best in club rugby, as the Saints won both the Lancashire Cup and Premiership Trophy. Neil produced a real scrum-half's masterclass in the latter at Elland Road and was a serious contender for the Harry Sunderland trophy, eventually won by Harry Pinner.

Despite his unbridled enthusiasm and commitment, it is a great pity that Challenge Cup final glory eluded him on two occasions, with the Saints losing by one point against Halifax (1987) and suffering a 27-0 defeat against Wigan in 1989, although Holding was by far the best Saint on view at Wembley that afternoon. He did produce a Man of the Match performance in the mud of Central Park in the John Player Trophy final of 1988, however, as his drop-goal proved to be the difference in a fantastic 15-14 victory against a powerful Leeds side.

Neil received a well-earned testimonial after ten years at St Helens and he played his last match for the club at Leeds in April 1990, when he appeared at stand-off. He was transferred to Oldham soon after, but re-signed for the Saints in September 1992, although he played no further first team games. He then coached at Bradford Northern and Rochdale, before concentrating on his job as a groundsman, initially at Knowsley Road and later at Liverpool Football Club's Academy in Kirkby. A brilliant mimic, Neil was a regular member of the Rugby League Roadshows of the 1980s, which did so much for players' testimonials. He remains a regular after-dinner speaker and was the on-pitch announcer at Knowsley Road for several years.

Sean Hoppe
Winger 1999-2002

Previous club: Auckland Warriors (New Zealand)

St Helens debut: 10 September 1999 v. Bradford Bulls

Final St Helens appearance: 25 October 2002 v. New Zealand

Appearances: 81+ 17 subs

Tries: 36

Goals: 0

Points: 144

Transferred to: Retired

Representative honours: New Zealand, Aotearoa Maori

A legend in his native New Zealand, Sean took part in seven major finals as a Saint, winning five, during his three years at Knowsley Road. Hoppe joined St Helens just before the 1999 Grand Final and was used in that particular match as a second-rower by coach Ellery Hanley, where his experience proved to be vital in Saints' 8-6 victory over the Bradford Bulls.

Prior to joining St Helens, Sean played in Australia for Canberra Raiders, Norths and returned home to the fledgling Auckland Warriors club (1995-1999). He scored a record 17 tries in 33 Test matches for New Zealand, and was an integral member of the 1993 European tour squad and the World Cup squad in 1995. He represented the Aotearoa Maori team in the 2000 World Cup and was named New Zealand Player of the Year in 1993, together with holding the seasonal try-scoring record for the Warriors.

Versatility and durability were two of Sean's greatest assets. His ability to slot into Saints' team in just about any position proved to be a vital ingredient in their Super League successes at the turn of the century. In Saints' back-to-back Grand Final victory over Wigan in 2000, Sean opened the scoring with a typically well-taken try. In the 2001 campaign, he formed a vastly experienced, yet nonetheless effective, three-quarter line, with the likes of fellow New Zealand international Kevin Iro, Paul Newlove and Anthony Sullivan. The club had its finest hour when they defeated Brisbane Broncos 20-18 in the World Club Challenge at Bolton, with Sean once again making a crucial contribution. The

side went on to win the Challenge Cup by defeating Bradford Bulls 13-6 at Twickenham. Sean's input in these triumphs was immense and only a crippling injury list ended any hopes Saints had of winning their third consecutive Super League crown.

The 2002 season was equally memorable for Saints' fans, with defeat in the Challenge Cup final against Wigan at Murrayfield countered by another incredible grand final success against Bradford Bulls. Supremely fit and never fazed under pressure, Sean played most of his football on the wing and proved to be the perfect role model for the younger players in the team. It was a blow to Saints' supporters when he announced his retirement at the end of the 2002 season, but there was a marvellous twist just before he hung up his boots. At thirty-one years of age Sean was drafted into the Kiwi side for the Third Test against Great Britain at the JJB Stadium, Wigan, on 23 November 2002. Although Great Britain won 16-10 to clinch the rubber in front of over 22,000 fans it was yet another highlight in a fabulous international career. He also played his final club game against New Zealand in a friendly just after the Grand Final – a fitting end for a true Saints' legend.

Lou Houghton
Second-row forward 1924-1931

Previous club: Pocket Nook Shamrocks

St Helens debut: 13 November 1924 v. Swinton

Final St Helens appearance: 26 December 1930 v. Wigan

Appearances: 233

Tries: 17

Goals: 0

Points: 51

Transferred to: Wigan

Representative honours: Lancashire, England

Once described as a 'big bear of a forward', Lou Houghton holds the distinction of scoring the first-ever try for St Helens in a Challenge Cup final at Wembley, against Widnes in 1930. He followed up a cross-kick from winger Alf Ellaby and was on hand to touch down. Unfortunately, his try came to nothing, as the struggling Saints were beaten 10-3 by a much livelier Widnes outfit. A local lad from Haydock, Lou signed from Pocket Nook Shamrocks on 4 January 1924, making his debut in the first team the following November in a 6-20 defeat against Swinton at Knowsley Road. Despite his size, he was a mobile forward, who went on to notch 17 tries in his career from 233 appearances.

The Saints had started to build a team capable of challenging for major honours by the mid-1920s and played their neighbours St Helens Recreation in the Lancashire Cup final at Warrington on 20 November 1926. In a rain-lashed encounter, the Saints were always in command and Houghton's unstinting tackling and work rate was a key factor in the first major honour won by the St Helens club in the Northern Rugby League. The Recs gained revenge in the League Championship semi-final at City Road, however, with a resounding 33-0 victory. After a mass brawl, Lou, together with his teammate Walter Groves and the Recs'

loose forward Mulvanney, was dismissed by referee Chambers. A fiery character on occasions, he could certainly look after himself on the field.

Lou was selected for Lancashire on three occasions, his first being against New Zealand at Mather Lane, Leigh, on 3 January 1927, when the Red Rose county recorded a resounding 28-3 success. His other county matches were in 1930/31, against Yorkshire and Cumberland. Lou also played once for England as a Saint, when they beat the Welsh 11-8 at The Cliff, Broughton on 6 April 1927, although he never appeared in any of the trials for the Australian tour in 1928. He won a Lancashire League winner's medal in 1929/30 but fell out of favour with the St Helens club halfway through the next campaign, when he was transferred to rivals Wigan for a bargain £325 fee, on 9 January 1931. Lou's last match for St Helens was against Wigan on Boxing Day. The club's wages book reveals he got paid £2 5s for the match, somewhat below that of star winger Alf Ellaby who received £7.

Lou was a member of Wigan's Championship-winning squad of 1933/34, although he missed the Championship final against Salford. He made ninety-six appearances for the Riversiders, including a further England appearance, against Wales at Huddersfield on 18 March 1931. A popular character, his transfer was met with much sadness among St Helens' supporters.

Dick Huddart

Second-row forward 1958-1964

Previous club: Whitehaven

St Helens debut: 18 October 1958 v. Workington Town

Final St Helens appearance: 29 February 1964 v. Warrington

Appearances: 209

Tries: 76

Goals: 0

Points: 228

Transferred to: Sydney St George (Australia)

Representative honours: Cumberland, England, Great Britain

In the late 1950s, the Saints' board brought in several fresh faces to heighten the strike power and crowd appeal of the first team squad. In the backs, two wingers were signed from South African rugby union – Tom van Vollenhoven and Jan Prinsloo – a devastating combination on the flanks. There was also second-rower Dick Huddart, from Whitehaven, who had shown such marvellous form during Great Britain's Ashes-winning tour Down Under in 1958 and St Helens were more than keen to obtain his signature. Like the famous petrol advert of the time, the Saints had put a 'tiger in their tank', and he remains one of the legendary figures in the history of the club.

The strapping 6ft and fifteen stone Cumbrian's greatest asset was the ability to take a pass on the burst and carve huge holes in the opposition defences with a devastating combination of speed and tearaway straight running. Add to that a jack-hammer hand-off, plus a safe pair of hands and it was not surprising that it took £7,250 – a record fee for a forward at the time – to bring him to Knowsley Road.

Huddart's barnstorming runs soon made him a big favourite with the St Helens crowd and he built up a fine partnership with Yorkshireman Brian Briggs in the second row. In 1958/59, the Saints were League leaders and lifted the Championship trophy with a marvellous 44-22 success over Hunslet at Odsal Stadium in front of over 50,000 fans. Huddart scored a trademark touchdown, with his characteristic hunched running style.

His Lance Todd Trophy-winning display at Wembley in 1961 will be long remembered by those who saw it, especially his devastating run that set up Alex Murphy for the first try. What a back row it was – Huddart, Don Vines and Vince Karalius. The 1961 final proved to be the pinnacle of Huddart's career as a Saint, yet he also tasted much success on the international front with two Ashes-winning tours with Great Britain. Indeed, he tore through the Aussies on their hard grounds in 1962 just like he tore through the best defences at club level back home on our more sodden turf.

Dick went on to win every honour with the Saints, including three successive Lancashire Cup finals, from 1961-63. He was transferred to the Australian champions, St George, in 1964 for a £10,000 fee and went on to win a Grand Final with the Dragons in 1966, against Balmain – no mean feat indeed. After a spell up country with Dubbo, he returned to England to play for Whitehaven, but soon returned to Australia and the Gold Coast, where he resides to this day. He remains a hero to the thousands who watched him play – a genuine Knowsley Road great. Dick's son, Milton, also won an England cap while with Whitehaven in 1984.

Alan Hunte

Winger, centre 1989-1997

Previous club: Wakefield Trinity

St Helens debut: 1 March 1989 v. Oldham

Final St Helens appearance: 4 October 1997 v. Brisbane Broncos

Appearances: 240 + 4 subs

Tries: 189

Goals: 0

Points: 756

Transferred to: Hull Sharks

Representative honours: England, Great Britain

Alan Hunte had all the attributes that enabled him to play anywhere in the back division, although he played the bulk of his rugby on the wing. He was a powerful, well-balanced runner, with good hands – ideally suited to the Saints' traditional style of fast, open football. A product of the Eastmoor amateur club, he signed from Wakefield Trinity on 1 March 1989 and scored two tries on his debut against Oldham at Knowsley Road. A confident, mature individual, with a touch of arrogance to his play, Alan became a first team regular by the 1989/90 season and played in a variety of positions ranging from both wings to centre and even stand-off. He scored 21 tries during the campaign, becoming joint leading scorer with Phil Veivers. Indeed Alan achieved this feat on two further occasions (1990/91 and 1997) and led the scorers outright in 1991/92, 1992/93 and 1994/95.

His career was occasionally blighted by injury, forcing him to miss some big matches and the dominance of Wigan loomed large in Alan's career. He played in seven major finals for the Saints, winning two – the 1992/93 Premiership final against Wigan at Old Trafford (10-4) and the incredible Challenge Cup final success against Bradford Bulls at Wembley, in which Saints triumphed 40-32. Yet Wigan won three Premiership finals (1991/92, 1996 and 1997), a Lancashire Cup final (1992/93) and a Challenge Cup final (1990/91), the latter despite a superbly taken try from Alan on the right wing in the sixty-first minute, reducing the deficit to seven points.

The son of former Wakefield Trinity winger Michael Hunte, Alan was always tremendously popular with the fans at Knowsley Road and, like his father, a talented cricketer. He played at the highest level in rugby league, however, representing his country on fifteen occasions, including selection for the 1992 Australian tour and the tour of New Zealand in 1996. He also played on the right wing in the 1992 World Cup final at Wembley against Australia, with his Saints' teammate Gary Connolly partnering him in the centre. Alan was selected in all three Tests against the Kangaroos in 1994 and in the Super League series of 1997, when he produced a dazzling performance in the Second Test at Old Trafford as Great Britain won 20-12.

Operating mostly in the centres, Alan was one of the Saints' most consistent performers in 1997, scoring 27 tries. Although Alan and his teammate Anthony Sullivan produced sensational hat-tricks in the 50-20 victory over Salford in the 1997 Challenge Cup semi-final, he missed the final when his injury hoodoo struck once more. At the end of the season, he was transferred to Hull FC and he later went on to play for Warrington (1999-2001), before joining Salford, where he has since joined the backroom staff.

Kevin Iro
Centre 1999-2001

Previous club: Auckland Warriors (New Zealand)

St Helens debut: 27 February 1999 v. Leeds Rhinos

Final St Helens appearance: 6 October 2001 v. Wigan Warriors

Appearances: 83 + 1 sub

Tries: 42

Goals: 0

Points: 168

Transferred to: Retired

Representative honours: Cook Islands

Born on 25 May 1968, Kevin Iro was approaching the veteran stage of his career when he was a shock signing by the St Helens club before the 1999 campaign. A powerfully built centre at over fifteen stone, with the ability to burst through even the tightest defences, he could also offload the ball in pressured situations, often using one hand, while he fended off the attentions of would-be tacklers. Iro was well-known to British fans, having enjoyed spells with Wigan and Leeds. He won three Challenge Cups with the Wigan club, together with two League Championships. After a spell with Manly, he joined Leeds, from 1992-1996, before joining the fledgling Hunter Mariners and later Auckland Warriors, on his way to Knowsley Road. He made his debut on the bench against Leeds at Headingley in a Challenge Cup tie, which the Saints lost 16-24.

Kevin was very much a 'big game' player, who would score vital tries when they were most needed. He formed a dynamic centre pairing in the St Helens' team with Paul Newlove and Kevin went on to score a vital four-pointer in the 1999 Grand Final against Bradford Bulls at Old Trafford that levelled the scores at 6-6 prior to Sean Long's magnificent winning conversion. Iro revelled in the Saints' style of fast, open football as the team repeated their Grand Final success in 2000 by defeating deadly rivals Wigan 29-16 in a pulsating encounter. Kevin's vast experience was utilised in the World Club Championship victory over Brisbane Broncos early in the New Year and the Saints completed a fabulous 'treble' by beating Bradford Bulls at Twickenham in the Challenge Cup final.

Universally known as the 'Beast', Iro will always be remembered in terms of the major finals. Yet he also produced some superb performances for St Helens in the Super League competition, particularly against Wigan on Good Friday 2000, when he notched a scintillating hat-trick in a 38-14 triumph. His second included a fabulous dummy, totally bamboozling Wigan's star full-back Radlinski. It was the Saints' first home win against the 'old enemy' since 1996, the first season of Super League.

Iro made thirty-four appearances for New Zealand during his career, playing in several Tests with his brother Tony. He announced his retirement from the New Zealand team and was selected as captain for the Cook Islands in the 2000 World Cup competition. Although failing to qualify for the later stages, the side finished with a 22-22 draw against the Lebanon – the first international to be played 'indoors' at Cardiff's Millennium Stadium. Always a name on the team-sheet to strike trepidation into the opposition, Kevin's power was sadly missed at Knowsley Road following his retirement in 2001, where he had achieved so much in such a relatively short space of time.

Mel James

Front-row forward 1972-1983

Previous club: Swansea RUFC

St Helens debut: 13 October 1972 v. Bradford Northern

Final St Helens appearance: 13 October 1983 v. Bradford Northern

Appearances: 305 + 16 subs

Tries: 41

Goals: 0

Points: 123

Transferred to: Retired

Representative honours: Wales, Great Britain Tour

Born in Resolven, South Wales – a fact often quoted by the late Eddie Waring during televised matches – Mel James emerged as the iron man in the front row of Saints' teams in the 1970s and early 1980s. Signed from Swansea RU club in October 1972, he operated at both prop and second row in his first season. At over 6ft and fifteen stone, Mel was supremely strong, a fierce tackler with the ability to offload the ball in the tightest of situations. Indeed, the ex-Swansea captain specialised in the hard graft of the 'first man in' during a set of six tackles. Yet Mel was to suffer an horrendous broken leg during the 11-7 victory over the touring Australians, in November 1973.

This cruel blow meant that Mel was sidelined for some sixteen months, eventually returning in March 1975, as the Saints were romping to the First Division Championship. Unfortunately, his nine appearances at the end of the campaign were not enough to secure a winner's medal. Thankfully full fitness was regained for the 1975/76 campaign, when the Saints picked up three trophies. Mel played in the BBC Floodlit Trophy final when Saints defeated Dewsbury 22-2 at Knowsley Road. He was the substitute forward in the 1976

Challenge Cup final, replacing John Mantle for the last thirteen minutes of a lung-bursting clash against Widnes. Yet he was to play a full part in the 'treble' bid, shortly after, in the Premiership final against Salford at Swinton, when his tireless running did much to wear down the opposing pack, paving the way for Saints' late surge for the trophy.

St Helens made it a Premiership 'double' celebration in 1977, with a magnificent 32-20 victory over Warrington at Station Road. Saints' rampant forward pack had laid the platform for success, with Mel James at the top of his form, scoring the final try for his team in typically determined style. He made a second appearance at Wembley in the 1978 classic against Leeds, when Saints' lighter, more mobile pack struggled to hold their Yorkshire opponents in the last quarter.

The Saints were rebuilding during Mel's last few years at the club, putting faith in a nucleus of young, local talent. His toughness was greatly respected by teammates and opponents alike and he was awarded a well-earned testimonial in 1982/83. He made his debut for Wales in a World Cup match against England at Warrington in 1975. Although Wales lost 22-16, James always wore the scarlet jersey with pride, making eleven appearances for the Dragons overall. Mel was also selected for the 1979 Lions tour, together with four of his teammates – Peter Glynn, George Nicholls, Graham Liptrot and fellow Welshman Roy Mathias. He did not make the Test team, but appeared in thirteen matches Down Under.

Les Jones
Winger 1967-1981

Previous club: Parr Juniors

St Helens debut: 24 March 1967 v. Wigan

Final St Helens appearance: 6 September 1981 v. Castleford

Appearances: 477 + 8 subs

Tries: 282

Goals: 0

Points: 846

Transferred to: Retired

Representative honours: Lancashire, England, Great Britain

Les Jones made more appearances on the wing than any other St Helens-born player and won virtually every honour at club level during his career. He appeared in sixteen finals for the Saints: two Lancashire Cup finals (1967; 1970), three Championship finals (1970; 1971; 1972), three Challenge Cup finals (1972; 1976; 1978), three Premiership finals (1975; 1976; 1977) and five Floodlit Trophy finals (1970; 1971; 1975; 1977; 1978). Although he may not have had the grace of Ellaby, or the agility of van Vollenhoven, he certainly had pace and was extremely difficult to stop when in full flight. Indeed, his try-scoring exploits for the Saints put him in third place in the all-time listings behind those two former legends of the three-quarter line – a fantastic achievement indeed.

Les signed for the Saints from Parr Juniors on 2 March 1967 and made his first team debut three weeks later against Wigan at Central Park, when the red-haired flyer scored a brilliant touchdown in Saints' 21-7 defeat of the 'old enemy', in front of a crowd of over 21,000. He earned his first winner's medal in the replayed Lancashire Cup final against Warrington in 1967, when the Saints pulled off a 13-10 victory, with Les scoring one of his team's three tries.

A county representative on eight occasions, Les had two particularly outstanding seasons at Knowsley Road. In the 1970/71 campaign, he played in 44 matches, scoring 39 tries – his highest individual total in a season for the club – as the Saints retained the Championship final trophy

after a closely fought match against Wigan at Station Road, Swinton. The 1975/76 'Dad's Army' season saw Les appearing in 48 matches, scoring 31 tries as the Saints were victorious in the Floodlit Trophy, Challenge Cup and Premiership finals.

Les won a First Division Championship medal after the Saints topped the table in 1975 with a nine point advantage over second-placed Wigan. His 38 appearances and 24 tries were one of the major reasons for the team's dominance. Indeed, the three-quarter line of the 1970s – Jones, Benyon, Walsh and Mathias, with Frank Wilson also in the frame – is generally considered to be one of the most potent in Saints' history, although not matched by the award of international caps for Les and his partner Billy Benyon. Les played just once for Great Britain, against New Zealand in 1971, when he was joined by his club colleague in the centre.

Les enjoyed a successful testimonial season in 1979/80, netting him a £21,000 cheque. He played 37 full matches for the Saints in his final season, in 1980/81, scoring 12 tries. He was, with Eric Chisnall, the last local link from the team of the late 1960s to leave the club. His achievements are the stuff of legend and he is a popular member of the Saints' Past Players' Hall of Fame.

Chris Joynt
Second-row forward 1992-2004

Previous club: Oldham

St Helens debut: 6 September 1992 v.
Wakefield Trinity

Final St Helens appearance: 25 September
2004 v. Wigan Warriors

Appearances: 363 + 19 subs

Tries: 121

Goals: 0

Points: 484

Transferred to: Retired

Representative honours: Lancashire, England,
Ireland, Great Britain

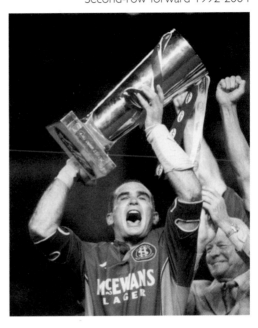

Definitely one that got away; that's Chris Joynt.
Born in Wigan on 7 December 1971, Chris
never played for his home-town team, going on to
achieve legendary status with their deadliest rivals
– St Helens. During his twelve years at Knowsley
Road, he picked up ten winner's medals and
appeared in fifteen major finals. He won the Harry
Sunderland Trophy on two occasions, was Man of
the Match in a World Club Challenge and played
twenty-five times for Great Britain, including two
Lions tours. Club captain at Knowsley Road from
1998-2003, he played in fifty St Helens-Wigan
clashes – more than any other Saint.

Chris signed for the Saints on 2 September
1992 after some superb performances for his
first professional club, Oldham. Indeed, his rise
to prominence came quickly, with a burgeoning
reputation as a hard-tackling and running second-
row forward. Who can forget his performance in
the 1993 Premiership final at Old Trafford, against
the team he supported as a lad, earning him the
coveted Harry Sunderland Trophy? The Saints
were the best-prepared team for the advent of
the sunshine Super League in 1996 and swept to
a glorious League and cup double – their first for
twenty years, with Chris a major influence for
those around him. The big matches came thick
and fast and the brilliant Wembley 'double' against
Bradford Bulls will long remain in the memory.
For Chris, in particular, the thrill of lifting the
Challenge Cup in 1997, despite club captain
Bobbie Goulding's presence, was an undoubted
career highlight.

Two years later, with Chris officially at the
helm, the Saints defied the odds and lifted their
first Grand Final trophy against Bradford Bulls at
Old Trafford in 1999. What a game it was, as the
Saints' pack stood firm and eventually overcame
their Yorkshire rivals – little wonder it remains a
favourite with supporters of recent years and they
have been spoiled by further success since. Apart
from Joynt's magnificent effort in the second row
there was Sean Long's incredible touchline conversion – one of the greatest kicks in the club's
history. We also remember the psychological effect
of the team coming out in those warm-up tops
with the red vee. It was a true masterstroke.

Then there was more to savour, with a repeat
success over Wigan in the Grand Final at Old
Trafford. Yet we will never forget the skipper's
unbelievable contribution beforehand, finishing
off the move that has been labelled the 'greatest

try ever seen in Super League history', against Bradford Bulls at Knowsley Road in the qualifying play-off – ten seconds after the final hooter had sounded. His ability to back up and get on the end of things had always been a major asset, with a fine scoring record for a forward.

He also broke the consecutive appearance record, held by hooker Harold Smith, that had stood since the late 1920s – another measure of his fantastic consistency. Indeed, it was success all the way in the new millennium, as the Saints followed their double Grand Final success with another victory, against Australia's finest, Brisbane Broncos, in the World Club Challenge, as the sleet and snow swept across the Reebok Stadium. Once again Chris Joynt was on hand to score a crucial four-pointer, but at some cost, when an ill-timed tackle hit him from behind after he had put the ball down – the price you pay for beating the Aussies, I suppose. Then it was down to Twickenham and yet another triumph over Bradford Bulls in the Challenge Cup final to clinch a marvellous treble success.

The 2002 campaign proved once again to be a triumph for Chris and his teammates, with another brilliant, nail-biting victory over the Bulls at the Theatre of Dreams. Sean Long's last-minute drop-goal was another for the memory bank as the Bulls

bit the dust once more. The last honour at club level for Chris was the 2004 Challenge Cup final at the Millennium Stadium, Cardiff, when the Saints defeated rivals Wigan 32-16 after producing rugby of the very highest quality during the run-in. By this time, Chris had handed over the captaincy to Paul Sculthorpe, but it mattered not one jot as he added yet another major honour to his incredible record of achievement in rugby league.

There have also been representative honours aplenty, including memorable victories over the Kangaroos and Kiwis, together with an amazing Indian summer with the boys from Ireland in the 2000 World Cup. Indeed, Chris has appeared at prop, second-row and loose forward for Great Britain, a measure of his great value in any position in the pack. He has also turned out at hooker at club level. 'CJ' was a talisman at Saints. Look at the times he took a well-earned rest on the bench only to be brought back to steady the ship when the team appeared to have lost their way. Chris has spent lots of his spare time helping others with organisations such as the Prince's Trust and his departure from Knowsley Road, after a successful testimonial in 2004, left a huge void. I suppose they didn't really mind too much down Bradford way, however.

Tony Karalius
Hooker 1967-1978

Previous club: Widnes

St Helens debut: 17 February 1967 v. Oldham

Final St Helens appearance: 8 October 1978 v. Rochdale Hornets

Appearances: 311+ 44 subs

Tries: 26

Goals: 0

Points: 78

Transferred to: Wigan

Representative honours: Lancashire, Great Britain

A member of a famous rugby family – brothers Vince and Dennis had played for the Saints before him – Tony was signed from Widnes in January 1967 and made his debut at loose forward. Although he was an adaptable footballer, his best position was hooker and it was over two years before he was to oust evergreen Bill Sayer from the No.9 jersey. Tony proved to be a marvellous exponent of releasing the ball in the tackle utilising his powerful arms and spade-like hands to great effect. A master of the bone-crunching 'Cumberland throw' tackle, his vision and tactical awareness close to the line were instrumental in securing points galore from short-range attacks.

After playing hooker for much of the 1969/70 season, fate intervened. Tony missed the 1970 Championship final through injury, but he was not to be denied twelve months later, as the Saints won back-to-back Championships with the 16-12 success over Wigan. His probing runs and defence were outstanding, especially after the dismissal of John Mantle greatly reduced the effectiveness of the pack. Tony managed to play in an incredible forty-nine matches up to the business end of the 1971/72 season, until disaster struck, when a groin injury prevented him from playing in the

Challenge Cup final against Leeds. It was a sad end to a campaign that had seen Tony's game grow from strength to strength, rewarded by county and international call-ups.

Tony was one of the creative hubs of a team that finished as First Division Champions some nine points ahead of second-placed Wigan in 1974/75. Karalius was also a member of the famous 'Dad's Army', who went on to lift three trophies during the following season; the BBC Floodlit Trophy and a fabulous Challenge Cup and Premiership double. He was in his element at Wembley against his hometown club, Widnes. In the sixty-eighth minute, he produced a typically brilliant 'long-armed offload' out of the tackle to send scrum-half Jeff Heaton roaring in for a crucial try. A justifiably proud Karalius scampered under the posts two weeks later, as Salford were defeated 15-2 in the Premiership final.

The emergence of young Graham Liptrot in 1976/77 restricted Tony's appearances, although he came off the bench to replace George Nicholls in the Premiership final against Warrington, for his last winner's medal as a Saint. Tony made five appearances for Great Britain and four for Lancashire. He was a key member of the Saints' success story of the late sixties and seventies and was duly rewarded with a bumper £10,000 testimonial in 1978. Tony moved on to Wigan, in October 1978, where brother Vince was coach, and later joined the fledgling Fulham club before finishing his career with the Cardiff Blue Dragons. In 2004, he was a worthy incumbent into the Saints' Past Players' Hall of Fame.

Loose forward 1951-1962

Previous club: West Bank ARLFC

St Helens debut: 2 April 1952 v. Warrington

Final St Helens appearance: 13 January 1962 v. Leeds

Appearances: 252

Tries: 42

Goals: 0

Points: 126

Transferred to: Widnes

Representative honours: Lancashire, Great Britain

Vincent Peter Patrick Karalius is a legend wherever rugby league is played. A member of the rugby league Hall of Fame, he skippered the St Helens club to success in the 1961 Challenge Cup final and repeated the achievement three years later with his home-town team Widnes. Vince made one tour Down Under in 1958 and came out of it as the 'Wild Bull of the Pampas,' such was the ferocity of his play as he helped Great Britain to bring home the Ashes. Mind you, Vince did not really mind what the critics called him, as long as his team won.

Born in Widnes on 15 October 1932 and one of seven brothers, Vince's grandparents were Lithuanian, his father Scottish and mother Irish. His early love was soccer, until he joined West Bank Juniors at sixteen. He was spotted by former Widnes trainer Peter Lyons, who was with St Helens at the time and signed in August 1951 for £200 after a couple of trial matches, making an impressive first team debut in a 13-5 victory against Warrington on 2 April 1952. Young Karalius had huge hands that enabled him to pop the ball out when seemingly engulfed by several tacklers, yet in those early days he felt the need to bulk up his twelve-and-a-half stone frame so that he could compete physically with his opponents. This he did during his National Service and weighed in at just over fourteen stone when he returned to Knowsley Road.

Vince was more a creator of tries than a try-scorer, but he had a fearsome 'bear-hug' tackle, as opposing scrum-halves found to their cost. He played the game hard and expected nothing less in return. Vince was the first-choice loose forward by the 1955/56 campaign, under master coach Jim Sullivan, when the team won the Challenge Cup for the first time, beating Halifax at Wembley. He had a superb all-round match that day, putting Alan Prescott in for the last try with a trademark pass from out of the tackle, despite nearly missing the big occasion after his ear had virtually been torn off in the semi-final replay with Barrow.

Vince's excellent club form saw him make his debut for Lancashire in their 42-21 success over Cumberland at Wigan on 6 September 1956, one of ten appearances during his career. He was also forming a partnership with a young scrum-half called Alex Murphy at Knowsley Road, which

was to figure highly for both club and country in the next few years. Vince was selected, with Murphy, for the 1958 tour Down Under. He missed the First Test, through suspension and made his debut for Great Britain in the Second at Brisbane, when the British won a famous backs-to-the-wall victory despite a crop of injuries that included Alan Prescott's broken arm. Although nearly crippled with a back injury himself, Vince put Alex Murphy in for a sensational try in the visitors' 25-18 triumph. A World Cup winner with Great Britain in 1960, Vince missed the 1959 series against the Kangaroos after a season plagued by injury. He managed two more matches against the Australians, in the 1963 series, with his final appearance at Swinton on 9 November 1963, when the Kangaroos rattled up a 50-12 success; a sad farewell for the Wild Bull in the international arena in his twelfth Test match.

Vince and Alex had starring roles at Odsal as Saints won the Championship with a stunning 44-22 success over Hunslet at the end of the 1958/59 season and it was Karalius who took over the captaincy following the retirement of Alan Prescott.

After steering his team to Lancashire Cup glory over Swinton, the undoubted highlight of Vince's career as a Saint came in 1961, when he skippered the team to a famous 12-6 victory in

the Challenge Cup final against Wigan, when the club's back three of Karalius, Vines and Huddart were exceptional. Yet during the following season, with ever-increasing work commitments to the fore with his welding business, he missed several training sessions, was stripped of the captaincy and transfer-listed. Loose forward Bill Major was signed from Widnes as his replacement and Vince, after 252 appearances and 42 tries in the red and white jersey, went in the opposite direction for a £4,500 fee. He galvanised the Naughton Park club and led them to glory at Wembley in 1964, before retiring as a player in 1966.

Vince proved himself to be a successful coach, with two spells at his home-town club, (1972-1975 and 1983-1984) bringing back the Challenge Cup on both occasions. He also coached Wigan from 1976-1979, although with somewhat lesser success. Two of his brothers played in the St Helens first team. Dennis made twenty-four appearances in the late 1950s and Tony was a stalwart at hooker in the 1970s, playing over 300 times and representing Great Britain. Vince was inducted into the Saints' Past Players' Hall of Fame in September 1990, with Alex Murphy, after the 1990 Centenary Match against Australia. The sustained and hearty round of applause that followed was truly indicative of his legendary status throughout the game.

Len Killeen
Winger 1962-1967

Previous club: Uitenhage RUFC (South Africa)

St Helens debut: 18 August 1962 v. Salford

Final St Helens appearance: 10 May 1967 v. Wakefield Trinity

Appearances: 187

Tries: 115

Goals: 408

Points: 1,161

Transferred to: Balmain (Australia)

Representative honours: None

Born in Uitenhage, Cape Province, South Africa, Leonard Michael Anthony Killeen was an unorthodox footballer and a brilliant entertainer. He could beat opposing defenders with sheer pace, a mesmerising body swerve, or kick over a helpless full-back and re-gather on the full on his way to the try line. He was also one of the sweetest kickers of a rugby ball Saints' fans had ever seen – his left foot was pure dynamite. Len was a man for the occasion – the bigger the better – capable of producing that extra something that would get his team out of the mire just when it was most needed! Killeen was a real laid-back character, who became a real favourite at Knowsley Road – and a Saints' all-time great.

A former First League baseball player, who represented South Africa at basketball, Len scored 25 tries in 27 matches in his first season (1962/63) and scored a vital try in the 1963 Lancashire Cup final against Leigh. He also won a Western Division Championship medal in 1964, yet Killeen really came into his own early in the 1964/65 campaign, when regular goal-kicker Kel Coslett was ruled out with a long-term injury. He duly obliged, with a mighty haul of 140 goals and 26 tries – topping the League charts with 358 points.

'Lenny the Lion' made significant contributions to Saints' famous 'four cups' season in 1965/66. His points-scoring, and goal-kicking in particular, were vital to the cause. In nine matches, Killen scored all his side's points. He kicked a last-minute winner in the League at Huddersfield; brought the Saints back from the dead in the Challenge Cup semi-final against Dewsbury with a sensational sixty-yard try and startled 100,000 fans at Wembley in the final against Wigan with a successful penalty kick some ten yards inside his own half. He went on to score a brilliant second-half try, following a perfectly judged grubber from his centre Billy Benyon, as he swooped on the loose ball without losing pace to dive over in the corner. It was to be only the second time that he was to handle the ball in the match, yet his phenomenal kicking earned him the coveted Lance Todd Trophy. A week later, he was scoring a hat-trick against Halifax in the Championship final, to complete a fabulous double celebration. He finished the campaign at the top of the try-scoring, goal-kicking and points-scoring charts – a fantastic achievement.

Len' success continued in 1966/67, when he finished at the top of the League's points-scoring chart for the third season in succession. Having won all major honours with the Saints in his relatively short career, he moved Down Under to the Balmain club in Sydney, where he won a Grand Final, against South Sydney, in 1969.

Barrie Ledger
Winger 1981-1988

Previous club: St Helens Colts

St Helens debut: 3 March 1982 v.
Featherstone Rovers

Final St Helens appearance: 15 May 1988 v.
Widnes

Appearances: 212 + 2 subs

Tries: 112

Goals: 79

Points: 601

Transferred to: Leigh

Representative honours: Lancashire, England,
Great Britain

Signed from the St Helens Colts team on 12 February 1981, Barrie Ledger soon showed why he is rated as one of the best home-grown wingers ever to play for the club. A natural footballer, great pace was his main weapon, yet he could beat his opponent in a variety of ways, using swerve, sidestep and change of pace. He also had the ability to draw defenders to him and then kick in-field towards the posts, leaving the cover flat-footed, before picking up and scoring under the posts. Barrie would also score some baffling tries when seemingly surrounded by his opposing winger, centre and full-back in limited space, he would put the ball down without anyone laying a finger on him. He was also a very competent tackler and is remembered as the man who came from nowhere to down Leigh's John Henderson when a try looked an absolute certainty, during the 1987 Challenge Cup semi-final at Central Park. If need be, he could kick goals too.

Barrie inherited much of his ability from his father Eric, who also played on the wing for the Saints in the 1950s. Despite some exhilarating tries, the young Ledger had to endure some disappointments early on, such as the 16-0 defeat

by Warrington in the 1982 Lancashire Cup final at Central Park. Ledger also scored a superb try at rain-soaked Knowsley Road against Wigan in the Third Round of the Challenge Cup in 1984, only for the Saints to lose 7-16 in front of a huge 20,007 crowd.

The 1984/85 season saw Ledger as one of the most dangerous wingers in the British game, as the Saints lifted the Lancashire Cup and Premiership Trophy, the latter in a classic contest at Elland Road, Leeds, where opponents Hull KR were blown away 36-16 by some brilliant attacking football. Barrie scored two cracking tries – both showcasing his searing pace.

The attacking tradition was carried on under coach Alex Murphy when the Saints scorched a trail to Wembley in 1987, with Ledger making 44 appearances during the campaign, scoring 23 tries. Yet luck deserted the Saints in the final against Halifax, when the side failed to produce the sparkling football of the previous rounds and were beaten by the more experienced side, with Ledger getting few chances to shine. He went on to score a try in the 1988 Premiership final for St Helens against a rampant Widnes side at Old Trafford, when an injury-hit Saints' side were belted 38-14. It was to be his last for the club, before his transfer to Leigh in 1988/89. A Lancashire and Great Britain representative, with two Test matches against Australia under his belt in 1986, he remains one of the most entertaining wingers ever to wear the red vee – simply unstoppable on his day.

Frank Lee
Forward 1899-1911

Previous club: Local juniors

St Helens debut: 10 March 1900 v. Salford

Final St Helens appearance: 23 December 1911 v. Runcorn

Appearances: 202

Tries: 15

Goals: 25

Points: 95

Transferred to: Retired

Representative honours: Lancashire, England

St Helens-born Frank Lee made his debut on 10 March 1900 against Salford, when rugby league was not substantially different from the code it had left behind. Teams were fifteen-a-side, with eight forwards. There were still line-outs and, as the marvellous footage shot by Mitchell and Kenyon at the turn of the century shows, there was a scrum after every breakdown in play, with forwards packing down on a 'first come' basis. Frank Lee was one of the most effective scrimmaging forwards around and a strong runner with the ball in hand.

In 1902/03, the Saints were relegated from the First Division after a miserable season, finishing second from bottom, with 9 wins from 34 matches. Keighley and Leeds replaced them. Twelve months later, however, the Saints had fought hard to gain a quick return to the top flight, yet tied in second place on forty-nine points with the Holbeck club from Leeds. The only solution was to have a special play-off match to see which club was to be promoted with the champions, Wakefield Trinity. The test match took place at Huddersfield on 14 May 1904 and special permission had to be obtained for the game to take place. Frank Lee and the forwards dominated a rather dour encounter, as the Saints clinched promotion in a 7-0 success. Despite showing top form, Frank had once again missed out on county selection.

There was more woe for the Saints in 1904/05, as they finished second from bottom, although the League was re-structured into one division for the

1905/06 campaign, sparing the blushes of everyone at Knowsley Road. The team finished in fourteenth place in the new Northern Rugby League, yet fell to unfancied Runcorn in the Intermediate Round of the Challenge Cup. It was Frank Lee's best season to date, however, as he was selected for Lancashire, playing in all three of the county's matches during the season, including a superb 8-0 victory against rivals Yorkshire at the Boulevard. This meant the competition ended in a tie, with Lancashire playing Cumberland in a play-off on 21 February 1906 at Wigan's Central Park ground – but this match also ended in a 3-3 draw. Frank also gained international honours with his selection for England against Other Nationalities on New Year's Day at Central Park, only the second international rugby league match played in this country. His teammate Tom Barton was also called up into the full-back spot as a late replacement. They became the first international representatives of the St Helens club – a landmark achievement.

Frank Lee went on to complete over 200 matches for the club, playing on until 1911. Like his contemporaries, William Briers and Jim 'Butcher' Prescott, he was a fine forward who gave his all for his home-town team in the early years of the twentieth century, in what were hardly the easiest of times at Knowsley Road.

George Lewis
Centre 1922-1936

Previous club: Pontypool RUFC (Wales)

St Helens debut: 25 March 1922 v. Featherstone Rovers

Final St Helens appearance: 20 April 1936 v. Barrow

Appearances: 428

Tries: 45

Goals: 850

Points: 1,835

Transferred to: Retired

Honours: Glamorgan and Monmouthshire, Wales

George Lewis and his brother Stan were signed from Welsh rugby union club Pontypool for a combined fee of £1,000 in 1922. Although Stan's career finished prematurely as a result of a knee injury, George became one of the pivotal figures at Knowsley Road. Playing mostly as a centre, he became the first to captain the club at Wembley in a Challenge Cup final (1930), lift the Championship trophy (1932) and was the first to kick over a century of goals (107 in 1926/27). He also formed a deadly partnership with wing sensation Alf Ellaby for many years.

Originally signed as a scrum-half, George was switched to the centres somewhat against his wishes, yet it was a move that transformed his rugby league career. Although relatively slight, George could time a pass to perfection and was durable enough to take any late hits from opposing defenders after he had got the ball away. An inspirational leader, who never gave anything less than total commitment to the cause, he played for Wales on two occasions in 1926/27 and also appeared for Glamorgan and Monmouthshire.

The Saints' team of the early 1930s was dubbed the 'Team of all the Talents,' with the likes of Ellaby, Fairclough, Mercer and Hardgrave giving them a real attacking edge. Yet the side lost the 1930 Challenge Cup final to Widnes. In a 1986 interview, George blamed a fixture pile-up for Saints' untimely demise:

We were licked before we started! We had 8 matches in 13 days. We won them all, but paid the penalty. At Wembley, we were heavy-footed. I've never felt so weary in my life. I found the turf was dead as well – but those eight matches were the real killer!

George was a creative, rather than try-scoring centre and in 1932, as a full-back, lifted the Championship trophy after a comfortable 9-5 victory over Huddersfield, at Belle Vue, Wakefield. One of the most enduring images in the Saints' history is of Lewis holding the cup, on the broad shoulders of big Jack Arkwright, surrounded by delighted players, officials and supporters!

George played on at Knowsley Road until the mid-1930s, before becoming coach for a season, but they were frustrating times: 'The club kept selling players,' he recalled, 'which was absolutely no good to me at all. In the end I packed it in and became captain and coach of the rugby and cricket teams at United Glass Bottles, where I worked.' He eventually moved back to Wales and the family home at Pentrepiod, near Pontypool – 'the house with the monkey tree.' George was an integral member of the Saints' team for over ten years, who always gained the respect of his teammates and was a real gentleman to boot.

Previous club: St Helens Colts

St Helens debut: 30 September 1973 v. Dewsbury

Final St Helens appearance: 17 February 1988 v. Hull

Appearances: 366 + 21 subs

Tries: 32

Goals: 0

Points: 104

Transferred to: Retired

Representative honours: Lancashire, England

Graham was what has become a dying breed – a hooker who could set up play from the acting half-back position and win the ball from the set scrums. He did both of these tasks superbly, coupled with an astute football brain and a great work rate. Local-born and signed from St Helens Colts, he made his debut as an eighteen-year-old against champions Dewsbury on 30 September 1973, finishing the season in his first major final, as Saints lost 12-13 to Alex Murphy's Warrington in the Merit Trophy competition. Although Graham played in the 1975 Floodlit Trophy final against Dewsbury, he did not become a first team regular until 1976/77, as a result of the consistency of Tony Karalius, and 'Lippy' ended the campaign as part of the triumphant Saints' side in the superb 32-20 success over Warrington at Station Road, Swinton.

The 1977/78 season was one of Graham's best for the club, with forty-three matches under his belt, climaxing in an outstanding individual performance in the Challenge Cup final against Leeds. Although Saints lost 14-12, Graham scored his team's first try and set up the second with a superb heel against the head for Bill Francis to sail under the sticks for try number two, giving his team a 10-0 lead. As the great side of the mid-1970s began to break up, Graham was a tower of strength for the next six seasons, enjoying a successful testimonial in 1984/85, when he won his only Lancashire Cup winner's medal, as the Saints, with

Mal Meninga in full cry, defeated Wigan 26-18 at Central Park. He made up a dominant front row, with props Tony Burke and veteran Peter Gorley, who established a steady stream of possession for an exuberant three-quarter line. Unfortunately, he was unable to play in the Premiership final at the season's end, as he had suffered the fourth broken jaw of his career at Featherstone Rovers, forcing him into premature retirement.

Graham did manage a much-awaited come-back, however and became an integral part of coach Alex Murphy's team that established a Division One record unbeaten spell of twenty-five matches, including the last thirteen matches of 1985/86 and the first twelve of 1986/87. He made a further appearance in a Challenge Cup final in 1987, against Halifax, yet like his previous match in the shadow of the twin towers, the Saints lost by the narrowest of margins. Graham was good enough to represent England on two occasions and won three caps for his county. His last match in the first team was against Hull, on 17 February 1988, when the visitors were thrashed 64-2, with Skipper Shane Cooper scoring a record-equalling six tries. It was Graham's 387th match for the club – a magnificent achievement, given his injuries over the years.

Stewart 'Steve' Llewellyn
Winger 1948-1958

Previous club: Abertillery RUFC (Wales)

St Helens debut: 24 January 1948 v. Rochdale Hornets

Final St Helens appearance: 15 February 1958 v. Oldham

Appearances: 287

Tries: 239

Goals: 0

Points: 717

Transferred to: Retired

Honours: Wales

Born in Abertillery, South Wales, Stewart or 'Steve' Llewellyn was originally too small for rugby and played soccer through school and at Caerleon Teacher Training College. He joined the Welsh Guards in 1943, seeing considerable action, including fierce fighting on the Anzio beaches in Italy and gained the rank of sergeant. Llewellyn started to play rugby after his demob, joining Abertillery in 1945/46, and was on the verge of moving to play for Northampton RUFC, when he caught the eye of the Saints' directors at a Monmouth v. Glamorgan county match. They went to sign forward George Parsons and stand-off Terry Cook and signed Parsons and Llewellyn instead, the latter for a mere £600.

Both Llewellyn and Parsons, who attended the same school in Abertillery, made their first team debuts at home to Rochdale Hornets on 24 January 1948. At 6ft and twelve and a half stone, Llewellyn reminded older Saints' spectators of the great Alf Ellaby and was soon a regular try-scorer with his change of pace and decep-tive body-swerve. He formed one of the best partnerships in the League with local-born centre Duggie Greenall and his trademark swallow-dive finishes over the try-line thrilled countless thousands of spectators during his ten years at Knowsley Road.

Arguably the best right winger never to play for Great Britain, Steve scored a try in both his Wembley appearances for St Helens, including a touchdown in the club's first-ever Challenge Cup success in 1956. Indeed, one of Steve's greatest moments was in the 1956 replayed Challenge Cup semi-final against Barrow, at Central Park, Wigan. His crucial try in extra time, with the match still scoreless, was the stuff of legends. He recalled:

> I received a pass from Glyn Moses eighty yards out before handing off Barrow winger Frank Castle. I turned infield and evaded the covering Reg Parker and John 'Dinks' Harris and by this time Castle had overtaken me, but I shook him off again and beat full-back Ted Toohey on the outside with thirty-five yards to go and then dived between the posts.

The very next day, Steve captained a reserve-riddled Saints team to a 12-9 win at Workington and scored a try for good measure.

A Welsh rugby league international, with four caps, he scored six tries on two occasions for the Saints – a record that has not been bettered. A tremendously popular and respected figure, he taught at Parr and Grange Park Secondary Schools in St Helens and, shortly after his retirement as a player, became 'A' team trainer at Knowsley Road for several seasons, before school commitments took over. Steve is a member of the Saints' Past Players' Hall of Fame and took a benefit in the 1954/55 season. He lies fourth in the all-time try-scorers' list, with only Alf Ellaby, Les Jones and Tom van Vollenhoven above him. Enough said.

Sean Long
Scrum-half, stand-off 1997-

Previous club: Widnes

St Helens debut: 16 June 1997 v. Cronulla Sharks

Appearances: 215 + 11 subs

Tries: 126

Goals: 782

Drop-goals: 11

Points: 2,079

Transferred to:

Representative honours: Lancashire, England, Great Britain

Sean Long's incredible achievements have undoubtedly propelled him to the status of 'all time great' at Knowsley Road. A superbly gifted footballer, with a touch of arrogance and a 'cheeky chappie' attitude, he has also been dogged by controversy during his career. Yet the archetypal 'big-match' performer remains a firm favourite with St Helens' supporters. A Wiganer by birth, Sean joined the Saints in an £80,000 deal from Widnes Vikings on 14 June 1997 and proved his worth immediately in the middle of a horrendous injury crisis. His first game was in the World Club Championship clash against Cronulla Sharks at Knowsley Road, when he kicked two goals in a 48-8 reversal. It was soon obvious that Sean would be a valuable acquisition for the club, with his electric pace, great hands and an astute kicking game. Sean appeared in both half-back roles during the rest of the campaign, scoring 7 tries and kicking 40 goals, including a fabulous sixteen-point bonanza in the 38-18 victory over Castleford in the Premiership semi-final.

Sean was able to renew his partnership with hooker Keiron Cunningham from his days as an England Under-16s international and he settled into the scrum-half berth with great aplomb during the 1998 season. In what was a time of rebuilding at Knowsley Road, with the departure of former skipper Bobbie Goulding, Sean proved his worth with 13 tries and 86 goals – with his deadly left foot notching ten goals in the League clash against Huddersfield. The 1999 season saw Ellery Hanley replace Shaun McRae as coach at Knowsley Road and Long was a key player in the Saints' side, forming a deadly partnership with stand-off Tommy Martyn. The Super League Player of the Year notched over 326 points, yet he also showed his toughness by battling the effects of a niggling shoulder injury and coming off the bench to score two crucial tries against Castleford at Knowsley Road to ensure a Grand Final appearance for his teammates. At a packed Old Trafford, it was Long who was the match-winner in a tension-packed encounter over Bradford Bulls. Coming on as substitute once more, he set up Kevin Iro's crucial try for the Saints. Yet it was his touchline conversion that won the day – one of the greatest kicks in the club's history. Sean was later selected, together with four of his teammates (Cunningham, Joynt, Sculthorpe and Sullivan) for the Great Britain and Ireland Tri-Nations squad at the end of the campaign.

Under Australian coach Ian Millward, the Saints retained their Grand Final crown in 2000, with Sean Long at the peak of his powers. He made 33 appearances for the club, scoring 420 points and lifting the coveted Man of Steel award. Sean was also involved in setting up Saints' greatest-ever try, against Bradford Bulls at Knowsley Road in the qualifying play-off, when Chris Joynt finished off an incredible sequence of play long after the final hooter had sounded. Long delighted the crowd by running around wearing the head of mascot St Bernard in the amazing scenes that followed. Sean notched twenty-six points in the next match at the JJB against Wigan, before the Saints beat their deadly rivals once more in the Grand Final, with Long prominent in setting up a crucial try for skipper Chris Joynt in the 29-16 success.

On a freezing night at Bolton's Reebok Stadium on Friday 26 January 2001, Saints beat mighty Brisbane Broncos 20-18 to become rugby league World Champions. Long's crucial drop goal, solo try and three conversions were an integral part of his team's triumph. But there was more to come, in the Challenge Cup final at rain-sodden Twickenham against perennial opponents Bradford Bulls, when Sean's brilliant kicking game earned him the Lance Todd Trophy and the Saints their eighth victory in the competition. Yet Long's incredible progress was halted at the McAlpine Stadium in a League match against Huddersfield, when he suffered a severe knee injury as a result of a late tackle. Injury was also an issue in 2002, although he was back for the run to the Grand Final and another clash with Bradford Bulls. In another incredible encounter, it was Long who dropped the winning goal with just over one minute remaining – the Saints' third Grand Final success in four years.

The 2004 campaign saw the Saints reach the Challenge Cup final with some brilliant football en route and it was Long who was a major influence. Yet the world of rugby league was duly shocked at betting revelations, concerning Sean and his teammate Martin Gleeson before a match at Odsal. A lengthy suspension followed for both players, effectively ending their seasons. Sean did play in the Challenge Cup final, however and produced a stunning exhibition of scrum-half play that earned him his second Lance Todd Trophy award, as Wigan were defeated by 32-16. One cameo, including a midfield break, chip and re-gather, and timely pass to enable Willie Talau to score his second try, was simply breathtaking in its execution. This is how Sean will be remembered when his Knowsley Road career eventually comes to an end. A real all-time great.

Previous club: St Helens Colts

St Helens debut: 1 April 1984 v. Oldham

Final St Helens appearance: 26 November 1995 v. Hull

Appearances: 286 + 11 subs

Tries: 80

Goals: 842

Points: 2,004

Transferred to: Bradford Bulls

Representative honours: Lancashire, Great Britain

Paul Loughlin was born on 28 July 1966; the same day that England's soccer team won the World Cup. Indeed he preferred the round ball game until his teens, when he played rugby union for West Park School and rugby league for the Hare and Hounds Under-17s team, coached by his father Terry, a former professional with Saints, Salford and Blackpool Borough. 'Lockers', as he is universally known, played for Lancashire and Great Britain Colts, signing professional forms for St Helens in July 1983.

At 6ft 4ins and fifteen stone, Paul was a real handful for opposing defences with his powerful running and – vital for a successful centre – the timing of a pass to put his winger away. He was a mighty 'downtown' kicker and goal-kicker supreme, who led the League's kicking charts in 1986/87 with 190 goals, some 73 ahead of his nearest rival, Paul Bishop. He began the campaign with a stunning club-record forty-point haul against Carlisle in the Lancashire Cup at Knowsley Road, including sixteen goals – another record in itself. The team reached Wembley, but lost against Halifax, despite a magnificent Loughlin try where he used his winger Barrie Ledger as a perfect foil.

Challenge Cup final glory unfortunately eluded him. He played in two more finals for Saints in 1989 and 1991 (v. Wigan) and for Bradford Bulls in 1996 and 1997, ending up on the losing side each time. Yet there were some outstanding perform-

ances for the Saints, such as his devastating two-try Man of the Match display against Leeds in the 1988 John Player Trophy and his try in the corner at Old Trafford against deadly rivals Wigan to seal a 10-4 success in the 1993 Premiership final. He also formed a dynamic partnership with winger Les Quirk, putting the 'Cumbrian Flyer' over the whitewash for 53 tries in 79 matches.

Paul played fourteen times for Great Britain and toured on two occasions, in 1988 and 1992. His most memorable moment was the try he made for his winger Henderson Gill, during the Third Test at Sydney in Great Britain's 26-12 victory – their first on Australian soil for fourteen years. Unfortunately, Paul's 1992 tour ended in injury, with a recurrence of a broken right arm, first shattered against Swinton in 1991.

Although he enjoyed a successful testimonial season at St Helens in 1993/94, he was transferred to Bradford Bulls, with teammates Bernard Dwyer and Sonny Nickle, as part of the deal that brought centre Paul Newlove to Knowsley Road in 1995. Lockers played in two Challenge Cup finals for the Bulls, losing to his former club on both occasions, although he did win a Super League title in 1997. No-one denied him that success. He remains an amiable giant of a man and a much-respected Saints' great.

Jamie Lyon
Centre 2005-

Previous club: Parramatta Eels (Australia)

St Helens debut: 11 February 2005 v. Widnes Vikings

Appearances: 30 + 1 sub

Tries: 24

Goals: 49

Points: 194

Transferred to:

Representative honours: Australia

St Helens Rugby League Club took a huge gamble when they signed Australian Test centre Jamie Lyon on a two-year deal for the start of the 2005 season. Jamie stunned the NRL by quitting the Parramatta club in Sydney just one game into the 2004 campaign after spending seven years with the Eels. Apparently unsettled by life in Sydney, the twenty-three-year-old returned to his home in Wee Waa and actually helped his local team to Grand Final success in the NSW Group Four competition.

The man who began his Parramatta career with five tries, together with a brace on his debut for Australia was tagged the new Mal Meninga by Saints' coach Ian Millward. Lyon soon proved his worth to the team at Warrington's Halliwell Jones Stadium in the fourth round of the Super League competition on 4 March 2005, when he was switched to stand-off half in the absence of Paul Sculthorpe. He engineered a stunning 18-16 victory by creating three tries in the last nine minutes. Apart from his beguiling handling skills, it was his kicking game that took centre stage that evening, with a brilliant 40-20 kick, followed by a spiralling bomb that was seized upon by Keiron Cunningham for the match-winning try with just a couple of seconds to go. Lyon's range of skills had to be seen to be believed, allied to deceptive strength and pace. His tackling technique was such that he could bring

down players much bigger than himself, such as the Bradford Bulls' giant winger Lesley Vainikolo. Jamie also developed an almost telepathic understanding with fellow Australian winger Darren Albert, the most explosive partnership in Super League in 2005. Most important of all, he settled down quickly into his new environment and clearly enjoyed his rugby once again!

Indeed, Lyon produced Man of the Match performances with regularity, scoring 24 tries in 31 appearances, as the Saints overtook Leeds to take possession of the League Leaders' Shield in 2005. Despite their 'great entertainers' tag, Grand Final glory eluded them, as injuries to key players took their toll. Yet Jamie produced a stunning individual performance against Leeds Rhinos in the Elimination semi-final to bring the Saints right back into contention with two brilliant solo tries, together with two magnificent touchline conversions in the last ten minutes. Although the game was lost 19-16 and the team were later eliminated by Bradford Bulls, there was to be some consolation for Lyon when he was named Man of Steel, the third St Helens player to receive this coveted award in Super League after Sean Long (2000) and Paul Sculthorpe (2001 and 2002). He was also named the Rugby League Writer's Player of the Year and Rugby Player of the Year in the BBC North West Sports Personality awards – due recognition indeed for a virtually instant Saints' great.

George Mann
Second-row forward 1989-1994

Previous club: Mangere East (New Zealand)

St Helens debut: 8 October 1989 v. Wakefield Trinity

Final St Helens appearance: 8 May 1994 v. Wigan

Appearances: 134 + 7 subs

Tries: 23

Goals: 0

Points: 92

Transferred to: Leeds

Representative honours: New Zealand, Tonga

It was Saints' captain Shane Cooper who recommended the signing of George Mann from the Mangere East club in Auckland to add some New Zealand beef to the forward pack. A former tourist to Britain with the Auckland provincial side in 1987, his powerful all-action style soon won over the fans, with a marvellous forty-metre try on his home debut against Featherstone Rovers on 15 October 1989. George was built like the proverbial brick outhouse and his bull-like strength was allied to great pace when in full stride. He could play with equal effectiveness in the front row or as a wide-running second-row forward, causing opposing centres no end of trouble with his barnstorming running style. He also had a penchant for the shoulder charge tackle and was renowned for his ability to offload the ball under pressure.

A New Zealand international, George had an absolutely storming game in the 1991 Challenge Cup semi-final against Widnes at Central Park, although the Saints lost in the final several weeks later to a patched up Wigan side. Yet his ambition for a winner's medal was fulfilled in 1991/92, when coach Mike McClennan's side beat Rochdale Hornets 24-14 at Warrington in the Lancashire Cup final, with George scoring two unstoppable touchdowns. He made 36 appearances during the campaign and scored 7 tries as the team finished in the runners-up spot in Division One.

However, 1992/93 was his finest season, as the club finished level with Wigan at the top of the table,

only to lose the title on points difference. George, together with his Kiwi teammates Tea Ropati and Shane Cooper, was magnificent in the 41-6 rout of the 'old enemy', Wigan, on Boxing Day 1992. At the season's end, Wigan were also defeated 10-4 in the Premiership final at Old Trafford, with George making some characteristic surges right into the heart of enemy territory. Surprisingly, he failed to score during his twenty-nine appearances, yet his powerful running and offloads were essential to the team's success. George was often used as a stand-off during a Saints' scrum feed, a tactic developed to generate fear and pandemonium among the smaller opposition three-quarters, which often succeeded.

The 1993/94 season was George's last at Knowsley Road, when the club failed to build on the successes of the previous campaign. He joined Leeds in July 1994 and appeared in the inaugural 1996 Super League competition, ironically won by his former club. George opted to play for Tonga with his cousin Duane Mann in the 1995 World Cup and featured in the famous Group Two match against New Zealand at Warrington that went to extra time, with only a Matthew Ridge field goal separating the sides at the final hooter as New Zealand snatched a 25-24 victory.

John Mantle
Second-row forward 1965-1976

Previous club: Newport RUFC (Wales)

St Helens debut: 23 January 1965 v. Whitehaven

Final St Helens appearance: 22 May 1976 v. Salford

Appearances: 422 + 13 subs

Tries: 69

Goals: 2

Points: 211

Transferred to: Salford

Representative honours: Wales, Great Britain, Other Nationalities

John Mantle was a real all-round sportsman in his youth. An Under-19s national triple jump champion, John could have signed pro-forms for Wolverhampton Wanderers and was his school's cricket captain before going to Loughborough College. He became shot-putt champion and captain of the rugby team, playing for British Universities, Leicester and Newport, where he was a teammate of fly-half David Watkins.

Essentially a No.8 forward, he represented Wales on eight occasions, including the 1964 tour to South Africa. At over 6ft and fifteen stone, he was seen as the ideal replacement for the legendary running second-rower Dick Huddart, who had joined St George in Sydney in 1964. Mantle signed for the Knowsley Road club on 1 January 1965, making his debut three weeks later at home to Whitehaven in a 16-3 victory.

Unlike some union imports, John made rapid progress, developing into one of the greatest all-round second-row forwards in rugby league. He possessed great pace and power, together with tremendous tackling ability and safe hands. John could also look after himself when the going got tough, making him ideal for Test match football – especially against the Australians. He was an integral member of the Saints' side that won four trophies – Lancashire League, League Leader's Bowl, Challenge Cup and League Championship – in 1966, when he showed terrific stamina, playing in no fewer than forty-eight matches during the campaign, relishing the emphasis on fitness that coach Joe Coan had brought to the club. Playing at loose forward, John displayed his power by crashing over for Saints' first try in the Challenge Cup final at Wembley, against deadly rivals Wigan, the result of a clever switch move involving Peter Harvey and Tom van Vollenhoven.

On 16 January 1966, he made his Great Britain debut against France in Perpignan and at the end of the Four Cups campaign he was an automatic choice for the Australasian tour, together with his teammates Tommy Bishop and Cliff Watson. John played his first Ashes Test at Sydney on 25 June, when Great Britain pulled off a fine 17-13 victory, although they later lost the rubber in the Third Test at the SCG by just five points. John had another crack at the Aussies during their 1967 tour, playing in the notorious 16-11 victory at Headingley and at the White City, where Australia set the platform for retaining the Ashes in a 17-11 success. Mantle did not tour in 1970, for personal reasons and made his thirteenth and final appearance for Great Britain at Headingley, in the Second Test against Australia on 24 November 1973 when the Kangaroos won 14-6. It was a pity that the start of Mantle's international career coincided with Britain's decline as a major force, reflected in the

dominance of the Australians – something that has continued to the present day.

John captained the re-formed Welsh team to victory against England at Salford in 1969, one of six St Helens players, including Frank Wilson, Graham Rees, John Warlow, Kel Coslett and Bob Wanbon, in the side. John played sixteen times for Wales, captaining them on three occasions and played his last game against England at Knowsley Road on 28 May 1978, when the Welsh were heavily defeated to the tune of 13-60.

By the early 1970s, John had won every honour in the game at club level. Initially a devastating runner and tackler, he graduated to the front row later on in his Saints' career, letting his handling skills compensate for his diminishing pace – and this despite a finger amputation! He was a major influence in the club's Championship-winning sides of 1970 and 1971, yet it was at Wembley in two Challenge Cup finals that he is best remembered. John played in the 1972 final against Leeds with twelve stitches in his head, as a result of a car crash; yet it did not stop him playing a major role

in the second row during the Saints' 16-13 success. In 1976, he had graduated to the front row in the famous 'Dad's Army' team that defeated Widnes. His grin of self-satisfaction on the bench after being replaced in the final few minutes is one of the most enduring images in Saints' history!

John and his Welsh teammate Kel Coslett went on to play their last game for the club in the brilliant 15-2 Premiership final victory against Salford – a fitting end to their careers at Knowsley Road. Indeed, John had appeared in an incredible nineteen major finals during his career, with Coslett just one behind. Always an extremely durable character, John went on to play more games than any other forward to come out of Wales. His last match was on 31 March 1982, when he scored a try for Blackpool Borough against Bramley. His post-Saints career had also taken him to Salford, Leigh, Barrow, Keighley, Oldham and the Cardiff Blue Dragons, where he met up once again with David Watkins. A former teacher in St Helens for many years, Big John is a member of St Helens Past Players' Hall of Fame and is firmly established as a true Saints' legend.

Tommy Martyn
Stand-off 1993-2003

Previous club: Oldham

St Helens debut: 5 September 1993 v. Salford

Final St Helens appearance: 2 May 2003 v. Halifax

Appearances: 188 + 23 subs

Tries: 127

Goals: 105

Drop-goals: 25

Points: 743

Transferred to: Leigh Centurions

Representative honours: Lancashire, Ireland

Born in Leigh on 4 June 1971 and signed from the Oldham club at the start of the 1993/94 season, Tommy Martyn was a footballing genius. A superb reader of a game, he could break down defences with a well-timed pass, a clever sidestep, a beguiling dummy, a cunning interception or by sheer deception – and he displayed a wide range of tactical kicks from towering bombs to the most incisive grubbers. He was the architect behind many of the Saints' successes in the early Super League era, bringing flair and creativity to the stand-off role that made him such a popular figure with the supporters. Yet he was an enigma. Tommy never played at international level for Great Britain and he had atrocious luck with injuries. He rarely played thirty matches in a season and recovered from reconstructions on both knees, three broken arms and several hernias – no mean feat in itself.

Tommy, together with Chris Joynt, Paul Newlove and Anthony Sullivan formed the most lethal left-side attacking combination in the game. The League and Challenge Cup 'double' in 1996 was followed by an immediate return to Wembley in 1997 against the same opponents, Bradford Bulls. Tommy scored two brilliant tries himself and made further touchdowns for Chris Joynt (superb reverse pass) and flying winger Anthony Sullivan (long, raking grubber kick) in the Saints' 32-22 success. Indeed, Martyn's fantastic all-round display that day earned him the coveted Lance Todd Trophy.

The signing of Sean Long from Widnes in 1997 saw the start of a partnership that was to take the Saints to further glory. They developed a near-telepathic understanding as a half-back pairing. When they clicked into gear, the team invariably played well. Tommy made 29 appearances, scored 14 tries and kicked 41 goals in 1999, when he finished the season off in style with a Grand Final victory against the Bradford Bulls. He won his second Grand Final twelve months later, against Wigan at Old Trafford, to add to a World Club Championship success, when the Saints beat Brisbane Broncos at the Reebok Stadium early in 2001. The Long-Martyn combination was typified by Sean's superbly weighted grubber in the 2001 Challenge Cup final against Bradford Bulls at Twickenham that was seized upon by his fellow half-back. It was Long's turn for the Lance Todd Trophy this time.

In 2001 he became the first Saint to score 100 tries and goals since Len Killeen in 1966, a record since shared with Sean Long and Paul Sculthorpe. Although Tommy missed the 2002 Grand Final through injury, he was voted the Super League Players' Player in 2000, representing Ireland in the World Cup in the same year. Tommy left Knowsley Road to become player-coach at Leigh in June 2003. His deeds typified what Saints' trademark 'off-the-cuff' style of football is all about. Long may it continue!

Roy Mathias
Winger 1972-1983

Previous club: Llanelli RUFC (Wales)

St Helens debut: 22 August 1972 v. Warrington

Final St Helens appearance: 24 April 1983 v. Widnes

Appearances: 390 + 21 subs

Tries: 218

Goals: 0

Points: 654

Transferred to: Bridgend (Wales)

Representative honours: Wales, Great Britain

A Welsh rugby union international three-quarter from Llanelli, who changed codes in July 1972, Roy Mathias was a natural rugby league player who had great pace in his early days. His powerful frame made him a difficult man to pull down when he got up a full head of steam – just like Tom Barton in the years before the Great War – and there was only one way for Roy – route one.

In his first season he topped the club's try-scoring charts with 26 tries, which included touchdowns in his first four matches for the Saints. His 40-try total in 1973/74 was the best for a Saints' player since Tom van Vollenhoven in 1961/62, including a hat-trick against Castleford, four tries against Workington Town and a fabulous five touchdowns against Rochdale Hornets – in successive weeks.

Roy topped the charts once again during the Saints' Division One Championship season in 1974/75, for the third successive year. He benefited tremendously from quality centre partners, such as John Walsh and fellow Welshman Frank Wilson, yet when Roy had the line at his mercy there were very few defenders who could prevent the inevitable. Although he relished the physical aspects of the game, he was a durable footballer and one of an elite band to have played more than 400 matches for the Saints, including every final reached by the club in that time.

He won a Challenge Cup winner's medal against Widnes in 1976 and his ability as a game-breaker was superbly illustrated by his amazing thirty-five-yard surge in the 1976 Premiership final against Salford, ending with a crucial try from Peter Glynn that turned the tide Saints' way – and a marvellous trophy 'double' ensued. Roy scored another fine try in the 1977 Premiership final against Warrington – his last winning final with the club.

Roy was a loyal servant to the club, earning a testimonial in 1983, by which time he had moved into the second row, as the Saints rebuilt their team around a nucleus of local talent. He could also draw on his vast international experience with Wales – Roy remains second only to the great Clive Sullivan, with twenty caps for his country. He scored a try on his international debut at Swansea, when the Dragons beat France 21-8 and he was an integral member of the 1975 Welsh World Championship team that produced some gutsy performances during the Australasian section of the group matches. Roy was selected for the 1979 Australian tour, after the withdrawal of Warrington's John Bevan and played in the First Test in Brisbane, on 16 June, which Great Britain lost by 35-0.

Roy has been a publican for many years and is a member of the Saints' Past Players' Hall of Fame. He remains fifth on the all-time Saints' try-scorers list, with 218 – and it will take a good 'un to shift him.

Stan McCormick
Winger 1949-1954

Previous club: Belle Vue Rangers

St Helens debut: 22 January 1949 v. Hunslet

Final St Helens appearance: 2 January 1954 v. Warrington

Appearances: 161

Tries: 99

Goals: 2

Points: 301

Transferred to: Warrington

Representative honours: Lancashire, England, Great Britain

The ambitious St Helens club paid a world record £4,000 transfer fee to Belle Vue Rangers to bring wing-sensation Stan McCormick to Knowsley Road early in 1949. A Great Britain international, Stan was a superb winger, with pace, sidestep and durability, who used to take part in professional sprint championships. He was also the master of the unorthodox and was famed throughout the game as the Interception King, scoring 16 tries from interceptions alone during 1947/48. His timing was sensational, lulling his opponent into thinking a crash-tackle was a near-certainty and as the pass came, Mac would suddenly step inside and pluck the ball out of the air and scoot away to the whitewash.

Born in Oldham in 1923, Stan played as a scrum-half for Lancashire schoolboys before joining Belle Vue Rangers in 1946. Although Rangers had internationals like Elwyn Gwyther and Doug Phillips, it was inevitable that McCormick would move on to pastures new. He scored twice on his Saints' debut at Hunslet – including an amazing eighty-yard dash to the line – and became a firm favourite with the crowd at Knowsley Road who marvelled at his jet-heeled acceleration and penchant for the unexpected. Yet his career really

began to flourish when the great Jim Sullivan took over as coach of St Helens in 1952/53. The side were runners-up in the Lancashire Cup and Challenge Cup finals, lifting the Championship trophy after a superb 24-14 victory over Halifax at Maine Road, Manchester.

The 1952/53 campaign was McCormick's best at Knowsley Road, with 38 tries from 47 appearances, including two superb touchdowns in the 26-8 victory over the visiting Australians – the Saints were the only club side to beat the Kangaroos on their tour – with McCormick performing one of his 'party-piece' interceptions in the twenty-seventh minute. Stan won a Lancashire Cup winner's medal against Wigan in 1954, yet it was to be his last in a Saints' jersey. He was transferred to Warrington early in the New Year and before the end of the season he was able to add another three medals to his collection, as the powerful Warrington side won the Lancashire League and lifted the League Championship and Challenge Cup, the latter after the famous replayed final against Halifax at Bradford.

After two seasons with Warrington and a brief flirtation with Liverpool City, he retired, before looking after the 'A' team at Knowsley Road in 1961. Following the sacking of Alan Prescott, Stan took over and guided the Saints to two Lancashire Cups and a Western Division Championship. Despite such success, he was replaced by Joe Coan and apart from a short spell at Salford in 1977 Stan had no further involvement with the game. A member of Saints' Past Players' Hall of Fame, Stan was a popular after-dinner speaker in his later years, entertaining people just like he did on the field.

Mal Meninga

Centre 1984/1985

Previous club: Brisbane Souths (Australia)

St Helens debut: 7 October 1984 v. Castleford

Final St Helens appearance: 11 May 1985 v. Hull KR

Appearances: 31

Tries: 28

Goals: 8

Points: 128

Transferred to: Brisbane Souths (Australia)

Representative honours: Australia

On 23 June 1984, Britain failed in their bid to capture the Ashes after defeat in the Second Test at Lang Park, Brisbane. St Helens supporters, however, received a most welcome consolation present after the game, when Mal Meninga, the giant Australian centre three-quarter became a Saint for the 1984/85 campaign. St Helens had paid around £30,000 for the privilege and with Meninga and his Brisbane Souths club-mate Phil Veivers in their ranks, the Saints embarked upon an unbeaten run which took them to the Lancashire Cup final against deadly rivals Wigan at Central Park. The 26,000 spectators who packed the terraces on that murky October afternoon witnessed a devastating first-half performance of awesome power and ball-handling skills as Meninga ruthlessly exposed the defensive frailties of Wigan's right flank. The sixteen-stone giant took less than seven minutes to make his presence felt. Taking Graham Liptrot's pass about fifteen yards from the line, he sold a brilliant dummy to John Ferguson before bulldozing his way over for Saints' opening try. Following tries by Roy Haggerty and Sean Day, there was more Meninga magic to come. A minute from half-time, the strong-running Paul Round looped over a one-handed pass to Mighty Mal in full cry. He handed off fellow Aussie Mark Cannon with contemptuous ease, leaving young full-back Shaun Edwards with the hopeless task of preventing yet more Meninga mayhem. Despite a Wigan comeback in the second half, it was not enough. Saints' 26-18 success was the club's first major trophy after a seven-year drought.

The club went on to become First Division runners-up and went to Elland Road to take on league champions Hull KR in the Premiership final. Once again it was Big Mal who took the plaudits, showing his tremendous power and pace to score two long-distance interception tries in the Saints' 36-16 triumph. Clearly, Meninga's presence transformed the Saints into a trophy-winning outfit for the first time since the late 1970s.

Mal never managed a second spell at Knowsley Road, for a variety of reasons, not least a succession of injuries, which disrupted his career for Canberra Raiders and Australia. Yet he remains a legendary figure in international rugby league, forever remembered for his awesome power, pace and handling ability. He could kick goals too – including a superb effort from the touchline at Thrum Hall in 1985, not that he attempted many goal-kicks for the Saints, mind you.

Indeed, the 'Wizard of Aus' is always assured of a fantastic reception every time he returns to the Old Dart, forever remembered as the man who kick-started the Saints' success in 1984/85; but let us not forget his fellow countrymen like Peter Sterling, Brett Kenny, Martin Bella and Paul Langmack who helped to make the 1984/85 season such a memorable one for British rugby league fans – especially those from Knowsley Road.

Bill Mercer
Centre 1924-1937

Previous club: Local juniors

St Helens debut: 26 September 1925 v. Batley

Final St Helens appearance: 6 November 1937 v. Warrington

Appearances: 311

Tries: 75

Goals: 0

Points: 225

Transferred to: Retired

Honours: Lancashire, England

William Napoleon Mercer signed for the Saints on 31 December 1924 from local junior rugby and played 311 matches for the club in the first great era of success from the mid-1920s to the early 1930s. A superb all-round centre, with excellent handling skills and a deceptive turn of pace, Bill scored 75 tries during his twelve years at Knowsley Road, picking up county and international honours along the way. He made his debut in the 15-3 victory against Batley on 26 September 1925 and soon established himself as a regular in what was becoming a real stellar line-up. Bill was to become an integral member of the 'Team of all the Talents' in 1929/30, which thrilled the crowds with its vibrant brand of attacking football. His partnership with New Zealander Roy Hardgrave on the left proved to be exceptional, matching the feats of Lewis and Ellaby on the other flank. Although the team won the Lancashire League title, they were beaten by Leeds in the semi-final of the Championship and by Widnes at Wembley in the Challenge Cup final, despite a magnificent individual performance by Mercer in the 22-10 semi-final success against Wigan at Mather Lane, Leigh.

One of the reasons for the Saints' demise was a backlog of club fixtures at the end of the season

– ten matches in twenty days in April – with several players involved in representative football. Bill Mercer made his debut for Lancashire against Cumberland at Whitehaven on 29 October 1929, with the legendary Alf Ellaby outside him, who raced in for three sizzling touchdowns in Lancashire's 15-7 success. Two more appearances alongside Ellaby, against Yorkshire and Glamorgan/Monmouthshire, brought further victories and the County Championship to Lancashire. Mercer made five county appearances overall and also played for England against Other Nationalities at Thrum Hall on 7 April 1930, in a 19-35 defeat, when Saints' Kiwi forwards Lou Hutt and Trevor Hall were members of the opposition.

Bill's domestic achievements continued by providing Roy Hardgrave the ammunition to score a staggering 44 tries in 1931/32, as the Saints won their last ten matches of the campaign to lift the Lancashire League trophy – the second such honour for Bill Mercer. Without the likes of Ellaby and Fildes, who were on the Australian tour, the Saints went on to become League champions with a superb 9-5 performance against Huddersfield at Wakefield Trinity's Belle Vue ground. Mercer picked up a loose ball on the left-hand side and fed stand-off Jack Garvey, who made the decisive break for Tom Winnard's brilliant match-winning try. Club captain in his later years, Bill played his final match for the Saints against Warrington on 6 November 1937 and went on to give many more years of service as trainer-coach to the 'A' team at Knowsley Road, where his knowledge and expertise was put to full use.

Glyn Moses

Full-back 1952-1959

Previous club: Salford

St Helens debut: 25 December 1952 v. Leigh

Final St Helens appearance: 28 November 1959 v. Leeds

Appearances: 259

Tries: 44

Goals: 0

Points: 132

Transferred to: Retired

Representative honours: Wales, Great Britain, Other Nationalities

Born in Nantymoel, South Wales, Glyn first joined Salford from Maesteg RUFC as a centre in the 1949/50 campaign, joining his elder brother Dai at the Willows. Glyn was very much a 'stormy petrel' in his early days as a professional and was sent off in one derby match against Belle Vue Rangers by referee Laurie Thorpe, when he retaliated after being kicked in the shins by Rangers' forward Doug Phillips. In the dressing room shortly afterwards, he was joined by brother Dai, who had 'got his own back' and had also been sent off. The evening paper headlines said it all: 'Biblical pair dismissed'.

Glyn became unsettled at Salford and returned to Wales with the idea of joining the fledgling Cardiff RLFC, but gave up the game when Salford refused to give him permission to turn out for them. Enter Saints' recently appointed coach Jim Sullivan, who enticed him back to the game for an £800 fee in November 1952. It was Sully's first major signing and a veritable masterstroke, as Moses made the full-back position his own with some storming displays. A supreme all-round footballer, he played in every match from January onwards and never drew losing pay until 25 April, when St Helens lost to Huddersfield in the Challenge Cup final at Wembley. There was consolation for Glyn, however, as the Saints lifted the Championship trophy several weeks later after defeating Halifax 24-14, in front of over 50,000 at Maine Road, with Moses himself scoring his team's final try. Always looking for opportunities

to attack, he was on the score sheet again during the 1954 Lancashire Cup final against Wigan, when the Saints won the cup for the first time since 1926.

His form for St Helens meant that international representation was a certainty. Glyn made nine appearances for Great Britain and represented Wales and Other Nationalities on two occasions. He was a member of the 1957 World Cup squad in Australia and toured Down Under again in 1958 with the Great Britain team that returned with the Ashes, but he picked up a knee injury that eventually led to his retirement from the game. He was a superb defensive player, who would use his shoulder to deadly effect to send attackers flying unceremoniously over the touchline.

Glyn was a member of the Saints' side that lifted the Challenge Cup for the first time, in 1956, after a pulsating game against Halifax at Wembley – the end of a fifty-nine-year wait for the club. He celebrated with two fellow Welshmen that day – winger Steve Llewellyn and second-rower George Parsons. A tremendously popular fellow, Glyn is a member of St Helens' Past Players' Hall of Fame, one of eight Welshmen with this distinction, including coach Jim Sullivan, the man who gave him a second chance for glory all those years ago.

Alex Murphy OBE
Scrum-half 1956-1966

Previous club: Local juniors

St Helens debut: 16 April 1956 *v.* Whitehaven

Final St Helens appearance: 28 May 1966 *v.* Halifax

Appearances: 320

Tries: 175

Goals: 42

Points: 609

Transferred to: Leigh

Representative honours: Lancashire, England, Great Britain

A brilliant footballer and the most spectacular scrum-half of them all, he won virtually every honour in a glittering playing career with St Helens, Leigh and Warrington and went on to become one of the game's most successful coaches. Alex Murphy was inducted into the rugby league Hall of Fame in 1988 and received the OBE in 1999 – a measure of his stature not just in rugby league circles, but in British sport as a whole.

Thatto Heath's greatest-ever rugby son was born on 22 April 1939 and the young Murphy was so promising in later years at St Austins School that he played in both junior and senior teams at ten years of age! Town and county honours at schoolboy level soon followed, delighting his headmaster and entor Gerry Landers.

On the eve of his sixteenth birthday, Murphy played in a final at Knowsley Road and was promptly whisked away by the Saints' directors who signed him on the stroke of midnight in the Pavilion at Knowsley Road. It was a tough apprenticeship. Coach Jim Sullivan made him endure seemingly endless sprinting sessions which laid the foundations for his success. Murphy made his first team debut against Whitehaven in 1956 and never looked back. A quicksilver half-back,

who had tremendous faith in his own ability, he was a shock selection for the 1958 tour squad, the youngest-ever Lions' tourist, playing in all three Tests against Australia and scoring two tries, as Great Britain won the Ashes. Two years later, he helped a powerful Great Britain side win the World Cup, scoring a brilliant try in the opening match against New Zealand at Central Park. Murphy had the chance to join the elite band of players making three trips Down Under, but it was not to be. Harry Poole of Hull KR was given the captaincy of the squad and Alex decided to stay at home to look after his business interests. He made 27 appearances for Great Britain, scoring 17 tries, although it could have been more.

Returning from his first tour, Murphy helped the Saints to victory in the classic 44-22 Championship final defeat of Hunslet, at Odsal in 1959, when he scored a sizzling long-range touchdown. The 1960/61 campaign saw Murphy at the top of his form, his supreme acceleration and pace bringing him a fantastic 32 touchdowns. He finished in fifth

position in the try-scorers' charts – unheard of for a scrum-half – with only flying wingers like van Vollenhoven, Rosenberg, Boston and Bevan ahead of him. A member of Saints' successful Lancashire Cup-winning side of 1960, Alex totally dominated the game against Swinton, as the Red and Whites cruised to a 15-9 success. At the end of the campaign, Alex made his first Wembley appearance in the 12-6 Challenge Cup final defeat of Wigan, scoring a try from close range after a fine pass from Dick Huddart. Murphy was an automatic selection for the 1962 Great Britain squad that retained the Ashes, although he suffered an arm injury on tour, limiting his effectiveness.

The St Helens team of 1965/66 steam-rollered all before them, with four trophies – the Challenge Cup, League Championship, Lancashire League and League Leader's Trophy – all ending up on the Knowsley Road sideboard. For Murphy, the most satisfaction came from captaining his home-town team at Wembley in the 21-2 success over rivals Wigan. He remains the only St Helens-born player to do so.

Regarded as the world's best scrum-half, he had played at right centre for much of the Four Cups campaign and a parting of the ways became inevitable. He joined Leigh, initially as coach – St Helens would not release his registration as a player – and then as player-coach, yet he resigned in

sensational fashion from Hilton Park after winning the Challenge Cup in 1971 and went to Warrington, where he repeated his Wembley magic by leading the Wires to another Challenge Cup win in 1974. Indeed his Wembley record is phenomenal – three wins as captain (1966, 1971, 1974) and four times a winner overall (1961, 1966, 1971, 1974).

Whether tangling with officials, like the imposing figure of referee Eric 'Sergeant Major' Clay or scoring a thirty-yard try, there was always something happening when 'Mr Magic' was on the field. He remained at Wilderspool as coach until 1978, when he joined Salford for the one largely unproductive spell of his career to date. Spells with Leigh (Division One champions) and Wigan (John Player Cup winners) followed before the wheel turned full circle and the prodigal son returned to Knowsley Road as coach in November 1985. Murphy's teams always played fast, open football and they made two Wembley appearances under his charge, in 1987 and 1989, although both were unsuccessful. The team did lift the John Player Trophy in 1988, after a marvellous battle against Leeds. Murphy left Knowsley Road in February 1990, replaced by Mike McClennan. Alex continued his links with rugby league in the Super League era with Warrington and Leigh, but he will always be remembered as the world's greatest scrum-half and St Helens' finest sporting son.

Frank Myler
Centre, stand-off 1967-1971

Previous club: Widnes

St Helens debut: 1 September 1967 v. Salford

Final St Helens appearance: 13 March 1971 v. Featherstone Rovers

Appearances: 139 + 5 subs

Tries: 46

Goals: 2

Points: 142

Transferred to: Rochdale Hornets

Representative honours: Lancashire, Great Britain

Before he signed for the Saints, in 1967, Frank Myler was a legend at his home-town club Widnes. A superbly talented stand-off half, Myler won every honour in his career at club, county and international level. He captained the 1970 Great Britain squad Down Under in 1970 and he remains the last visiting captain to come away with the Ashes, after a 2-1 success in the rubber. Frank also won a Challenge Cup winners' medal with Widnes in 1964, scoring a typical opportunist try under the posts.

Myler joined the Saints in 1967, essentially as a centre, with forwards Ray French and Dave Markey going to Naughton Park in exchange. He provided the perfect link between the backs and forwards – and he could still score tries. Frank got himself into the record books as one of only five St Helens' players to score six tries in a match, a feat he accomplished with ease against amateurs Maryport, in a Lancashire Cup clash in September 1969. Yet there were bigger fish to fry before the end of the campaign, as the Saints played Leeds in the Championship final at Odsal. Myler was superb, showing his silky skills both in attack and defence. It was a performance that earned him the coveted Harry Sunderland Trophy as Man of the Match and cemented his place in the 1970 Australian tour

squad as captain. It was quite a shock for the un-assuming, thirty-one-year-old veteran when details were announced. Yet Myler and vice captain Cliff Watson (his teammate at Knowsley Road) proved that the selectors had got it spot on, and Myler's superb displays in the centre in all six Tests Down Under were crucial to the team's success.

Frank retained the captaincy for the 1970 World Cup, held in England, but Australia gained consolation for their Ashes loss by winning the competition. For Myler it had been a fabulous Indian summer of international football, bringing his total appearances for Great Britain to two dozen. Frank won a Lancashire Cup winner's medal after the Saints' 30-2 thrashing of Oldham in 1968/69 at Central Park, together with a Lancashire League winner's medal at the end of the campaign. He appeared in two losing Floodlit Trophy finals and was in the side that lost the Lancashire Cup final to Leigh in the 1970/71 campaign.

Frank joined Rochdale Hornets as player-coach (May 1971-May 1974), together with coaching spells at Widnes (1975-1978), Swinton (January 1980-May 1981) and Oldham (1981-1983). He also coached at international level, including England (1977/78) and Great Britain (1982-1984); including the 1984 Australian tour, although Britain failed to bring the Ashes home after three straight losses against the Aussies. It is a pity that Myler came to Knowsley Road relatively late in his career, yet his deeds for club and country in 1970 will never be forgotten.

Paul Newlove
Centre 1995-2003

Previous club: Bradford Bulls

St Helens debut: 3 December 1995 *v.* Workington Town

Final St Helens appearance: 3 October 2003 *v.* Wigan Warriors

Appearances: 208

Tries: 134

Goals: 0

Points: 536

Transferred to: Castleford

Representative honours: England, Great Britain

Who could ever forget that magnificent night at the Reebok Stadium in 2001, when the Saints beat the might of Brisbane Broncos 20-18 to lift the coveted World Club Challenge trophy? It was 12-18 to the Australians in the fifty-first minute as the hail and sleet filled the sky. Hooker Keiron Cunningham surged almost to halfway, Sean Long took it on and played a superb cut-out pass to Paul Newlove in the left centre position on halfway. Aussie winger Wendell Sailor had come up too quickly and Newlove, the master centre, shimmied and went past his opponent on the inside – a superb piece of footwork for such a big man. As full-back Lockyer moved up, Paul threw a perfect pass inside to the supporting Chris Joynt who completed the touchdown from twenty-five metres. The Saints were level with the conversion. It set up the platform for the team's eventual triumph and illustrated the importance of Newlove to the Saints' success, particularly in the first five years of Super League. Indeed, Paul had also tackled brilliantly during the eighty minutes – an aspect of his game that has tended to be overlooked in comparison to his marvellous attacking skills.

Naturally shy and unassuming, Newlove was the last piece in Saints' team-building ready for the assault on the inaugural Super League competition. Signed from Bradford Bulls, Paul cost a world record £500,000 fee, including Bernard Dwyer, Sonny Nickle and Paul Loughlin transferred to Odsal as part of the deal. He was the big star, revealed to the St Helens public coming out of a security van before the press conference, on 29 November 1995 – and he did not disappoint. Naturally strong and a superbly balanced runner in full flight, he was a sensational strike centre, with the traditional centre's ability to put his winger away with a well-timed pass. His timing was so good that he was a master of the interception, capable of scoring tries from any distance. In his first full season in Super League, he helped the Saints to the League and Challenge Cup 'double', with his own contribution an astounding 36 tries from 27 appearances, a record only surpassed in 2004, by Leeds' Danny Maguire. Paul presented him with a trophy for achieving this feat.

Born in Featherstone on 10 August 1971, Paul was a member of a famous rugby league family, including his father John, who played for Rovers and his uncle, Charlie Stone, a legendary player with Hull. Paul began his career with the Rovers, where he won a Second Division Championship

medal and broke the club's try-scoring record. He also made a record eight appearances for Great Britain Under-21s and became the youngest Great Britain international, in the Second Test against New Zealand at Elland Road on 28 October 1989, at the age of eighteen years and seventy-two days. Newlove was selected for the 1992 Great Britain tour Down Under and played in the Second Test at Melbourne, which the visitors won 33-10. By now a hot property, Paul joined Bradford Northern for £245,000 on 13 July 1993 and took part in the 1995 World Cup before his move to St Helens, where his career really took off. He won four Super League titles, three Challenge Cups and a World Club Championship with the Saints, despite a round trip of 130 miles to get to Knowsley Road every day.

The 1997 campaign saw a successful return to Wembley for Paul, with a 32-22 victory over the Bradford Bulls, yet the team was plagued by injuries and failed to make an impression in the league-based World Club Championships. Newlove did play in all three Super League Tests against the visiting Australians, but the British lost the rubber once more by 2-1. Despite failing to win a major honour in Super League for the first time, Paul still scored 19 tries in 28 appearances in 1998, including a sensational match against London Broncos at the Stoop, when he put Anthony Sullivan in for five touchdowns in a stunning 37-22 success.

Paul was joined in the centres by New Zealander Kevin Iro in 1999 and played in his first Grand Final, against Bradford Bulls. Although the tries kept on coming, he was unlucky to miss the 2000 final against Wigan as a result of illness. Tragedy was to strike in the game at the Boulevard, on 2 July 2001, when Paul ruptured his achilles tendon, an injury that took many months to heal. Despite what was a particularly hard road back to fitness, Paul once again was able to play at Super League level, after intense physiotherapy and rehab over nine months.

The team came back from the disappointment of a Challenge Cup loss to Wigan in 2002 to beat Bradford Bulls in the Grand Final, with a late drop-goal from Sean Long. Newlove helped to create that opportunity with a midfield burst in what was his last major final for the club. At the end of 2003, he joined Castleford for a spell before injury got the better of him and retirement beckoned – the end of a marvellous career in rugby league generally and as a Saint in particular.

George Nicholls

Second-row forward 1973-1981

Previous club: Widnes

St Helens debut: 20 January 1973 v. Leeds

Final St Helens appearance: 21 April 1981 v. Widnes

Appearances: 266 + 6 subs

Tries: 41

Goals: 0

Points: 123

Transferred to: Cardiff Blue Dragons

Honours: Lancashire, England, Great Britain

George Nicholls is one of the greatest-ever second-row forwards in rugby league history – and certainly one of the most decorated. His play was characterised by phenomenal tackling ability, great handling skills and dynamic running power – he had it all, bar a kicking game. George signed for his home-town club Widnes from the Derby Arms club in 1966 and soon established himself in the first team at Naughton Park. He made a Lancashire Cup final and Floodlit Trophy final appearance for the Chemics, but ended up on the losing side on both occasions, yet county and international honours came his way, with George making his debut for Great Britain against the visiting Kiwis in 1971. He also played in all four games during Great Britain's successful World Cup campaign in 1972, in France. In the drawn final against Australia at Lyons, it was a tremendous cover tackle by Nicholls near his own line which saved a certain try and jolted the ball loose. Winger Clive Sullivan picked up and raced eighty yards for a sensational touchdown, pursued in vain by half a dozen breathless Kangaroos.

He proved to be a major transfer coup for St Helens at the start of the 1972/73 season, when his international quality and overall consistency

did much to boost the club's forward power in the continuing quest for honours. On the international front Nicholls strode like a colossus, despite a decade in which Great Britain sank from Ashes-winning glory in 1970 to an Australian whitewash nine years later. He was an automatic choice for his country when fit, playing against the 1973 Australian tourists in two Tests, before joining the Great Britain party for the tour Down Under in 1974, with his club colleagues Dave Eckersley and Eric Chisnall. Great Britain lost the series 2-1, yet the margins of defeat were close. George also took part in the 1975 World Cup competition with England, which once again was held in Australia.

George returned to Australia for the 1977 World Cup competition and continued his combat with the Aussies in 1978. He made his fourth visit to Australia in just five years with his selection for the Great Britain squad in 1979, when he was appointed captain, following Doug Laughton's return home after just one Test match. He turned out at prop in five of the six Test matches and proved as durable as ever. His last Test was against New Zealand at Auckland on 11 August 1979, when the home side lost 18-11, although Britain clinched the rubber 2-1. George

made 29 appearances for Great Britain overall, just one match fewer than fellow Saint Cliff Watson, the most capped forward – a wonderful record of consistency.

George blazed a silver trail with his club in the 1970s, with the Saints lifting the First Division Championship in grand style in 1975, although they lost out in the Premiership final against Leeds at Central Park. The 1975/76 campaign was one of George's finest at club level, beginning with a Floodlit Trophy success against Dewsbury at Knowsley Road. Yet this was overshadowed at the end of the campaign with marvellous Challenge Cup and Premiership Trophy victories for what was dubbed a 'Dad's Army' side. George kept driving the pack on at Wembley against Widnes, but his performance in the Premiership final against Salford was awe-inspiring, when his well-timed pass put stand-off Peter Glynn over for a crucial touchdown that turned the game St Helens' way. He received the Harry Sunderland Trophy later as the Man of the Match and helped the Saints to win back-to-back Premierships the following season, as Warrington were defeated by 32-20 at Station Road, Swinton.

Nicholls was at his brilliant best during the 1978 Jubilee Challenge Cup final against Leeds, when the Saints surged into a 10-0 lead courtesy of tries from Liptrot and Francis, together with two Pimblett goals. Despite Nicholls constant probing and incessant tackling, the heavier Leeds pack gradually got on top to win by two drop-goals in the last five minutes. It was a superb final and Nicholls was the worthy winner of the Lance Todd Trophy, to go with the Harry Sunderland Trophy picked up in 1976, a double award George shares with his teammate Geoff Pimblett. In the same season George was also voted the Trumann's Man of Steel and the Division One Player of the Year to add to his long list of achievements in the game.

The Saints were going through a rebuilding phase in the early 1980s and George was rewarded with a testimonial at Knowsley Road in 1981 before the old warhorse finished a memorable sixteen-year career with a short spell at the newly formed Cardiff Blue Dragons club in 1981/82, where he linked up with several of his former teammates, including Ken Gwilliam, Tony Karalius and Frank Wilson. He remains one of the greatest players ever to wear the famous red vee and is a member of St Helens' Past Players' Hall of Fame; a player who gave his all for club and country.

Sonny Nickle

Front row, second-row forward 1991-1995/1999-2001/2001-2002

Previous club: Sheffield Eagles

St Helens debut: 1 September 1991 v. Hull

Final St Helens appearance: 5 October 2002 v. Bradford Bulls

Appearances: 206 + 26 subs

Tries: 49

Goals: 0

Points: 196

Transferred to: Bradford Bulls (first spell), Barrow (second spell) and Leigh (third spell)

Representative honours: England, Great Britain

Seeing the name Sonny Nickle on the team-sheet was bad news for the opposition. Terrifically strong, he was the archetypal blockbusting second-row forward when he first came to Knowsley Road in an £80,000 deal from Sheffield Eagles in 1991. At over 6ft and seventeen stone he was very much the enforcer of the Saints' pack, so difficult to bring down and such a vigorous and enthusiastic tackler.

Sonny was a member of the Saints' Premiership final side that lost 48-16 against deadly rivals Wigan in 1992 at Old Trafford and was a selected for the Great Britain tour Down Under at the end of the season. The 1992/93 campaign saw St Helens come so close to challenging Wigan successfully for major honours and Nickle had a starring role in the Premiership final, where the Saints pulled off a marvellous 10-4 victory, gaining due revenge for the previous season's demise. The Saints never really built on their success however and as part of the preparations for the forthcoming summer Super League, Sonny was transferred to Bradford in November 1995, together with teammates Bernard Dwyer and Paul Loughlin, as part of the deal that brought star centre Paul Newlove to Knowsley Road.

Ironically, Sonny found himself playing against his former club in the 1996 Challenge Cup final. Despite his efforts, the Saints won a memorable 40-32 victory in one of the greatest matches played at Wembley. He was there again twelve months later, only to be beaten by his former club once again, although Bradford did win the League competition.

It was a veritable masterstroke to bring him back to St Helens for the 1999 season under coach Ellery Hanley. Sonny won a Grand Final winner's medal at the end of the campaign, against his former Bradford teammates. Now equally at home as a front-rower, he helped the club to retain the Super League trophy in 2000, as Wigan were beaten 29-16 and picked up a World Club Championship winner's medal after the Saints' victory over Brisbane Broncos. His last honour for the club was in the 2001 Challenge Cup final, when the Saints defeated Bradford Bulls once more – a somewhat recurring theme in his career.

In a somewhat bizarre situation, he was transferred to Barrow at the end of the 2001 season, yet never played for the Cumbrian club. He was still under suspension for a tackle on Leeds' hooker Robbie Mears and he re-joined the Saints for the third time, before the suspension had been served. Sonny's 'go-forward' was still in evidence in the 2002 campaign, although he was unlucky not to be selected for the Grand Final against Bradford Bulls. A popular character, Sonny signed for Leigh Centurions on 30 December 2002, just grateful for that extra season at Knowsley Road.

George Parsons
Second-row forward 1947-1957

Previous club: Abertillery RUFC (Wales)

St Helens debut: 24 January 1948 v. Rochdale Hornets

Final St Helens appearance: 6 April 1957 v. Leeds

Appearances: 296

Tries: 45

Goals: 40

Points: 215

Transferred to: Rochdale Hornets

Representative honours: Wales, Great Britain (Non Test status)

Born in Newbridge, South Wales, on 21 April 1926 – the same day as the Queen – he spent most of his early life in Abertillery. George started to play rugby at grammar school and as a sixteen-year-old was selected for Cardiff RUFC. He would play for his school in the morning and club in the afternoon! At seventeen he was playing for Newport and made such progress that he was capped for Wales aged nineteen – the youngest forward ever to play in an international at the time.

Called up in 1944, George served with the Royal Welsh Fusiliers, but obtained a Class B release to join the police, serving with the force for ten months, but decided he preferred the army. His superintendent, an official of the Pontypool club, phoned the Welsh RFU to tell them that it was because he was about to turn professional. As a result, he was asked to leave the Welsh international party while they were travelling by train to Paris and was suspended for six weeks. Although he was reinstated, Saints signed him in December 1947, together with teammate Steve Llewellyn, from his new club Abertillery. Prior to this he had been approached by no fewer than twenty-two rugby league clubs, but certainly made the right

choice in the end. A fast, clever second-rower and one of the best-ever recruits from the union code, George's career blossomed under coach Jim Sullivan. He appeared at Wembley in Saints' defeat against Huddersfield, yet had the consolation of picking up a League Championship and Lancashire League winner's medal the same season, as Sullivan's methods started to take effect. In 1953 he was in the side that beat rivals Wigan 16-8 in the final of the Lancashire Cup in front of 42,793 spectators at Station Road, Swinton. In 1956, George was in the second row as the Saints won the Challenge Cup for the first time, in a titanic clash against Halifax, having scored a crucial try in the semi-final replay with Barrow.

George played twelve times for Wales, playing his last game for the Principality against France in a 22-23 defeat at Marseilles – the last international played by Wales for the next fifteen years. Parsons played for Great Britain against an Australian XIII in 1951 as part of the Festival of Britain celebrations.

He left St Helens in October 1957 to become player-coach at Rochdale Hornets and got the Lancashire side to the Challenge Cup semi-final in 1957/58 only to lose 3-5 to a powerful Wigan outfit. Twelve months later he moved to Salford as player-coach and stayed for three years before retiring at the age of thirty-five. Now back living in South Wales, he is a proud member of the Saints' Past Player Association's Hall of Fame – a worthy commendation for a great player and a real gentleman.

Apollo Perelini

Front-row forward 1994-2000

Previous club: North Harbour RUFC (New Zealand)

St Helens debut: 11 September 1994 v. Workington Town

Final St Helens appearance: 14 October 2000 v. Wigan Warriors

Appearances: 163 + 30 subs

Tries: 44

Goals: 0

Points: 176

Transferred to: Sale Sharks RUFC

Representative honours: Western Samoa

A genuine Super League legend, Apollo Perelini was born in Samoa on 16 July 1969 and moved with his family to New Zealand at the age of three. He was named after the famous American space mission, featuring Neil Armstrong's walk on the moon and his middle name is actually Eleven! At over 6ft and seventeen stone, Apollo was a natural rugby player and went on to represent the Junior All Blacks. He was not considered for the 1991 senior World Cup squad, however and elected to play for Samoa in the competition. In the match against Wales in Cardiff, he promptly dispatched three Welshmen from the game with a series of devastating tackles.

Apollo had previously turned down approaches from rugby league clubs, including Australian club Manly. He joined the professional ranks with St Helens on 3 June 1994, however, scoring his first try in a 22-22 draw at Batley in a Regal Trophy tie. Apollo soon adapted to the demands of the thirteen-a-side code and represented Samoa in the Centenary Rugby League World Cup in 1995, with his teammate Vila Matautia.

The Saints became a real power during the first season of the new summer Super League in 1996, winning the League by a single point from rivals Wigan and lifting the Challenge Cup after one of the most sensational matches ever seen at Wembley. Perelini's mobility and tackling power made him an integral member of the team typified by his late try at The Valley against London Broncos that helped to keep his club in the title race. A deeply religious man,

he scored Saints' eighth and final try at Wembley against the Bradford Bulls in a fabulous 40-32 success and paused to give a prayer of thanks before being engulfed by his joyful teammates. Apollo was later named in the Stones Bitter 'dream team', together with his teammates Paul Newlove, Anthony Sullivan, Bobbie Goulding and Keiron Cunningham. He was also the Rugby League Writers' Player of the Year – another fantastic achievement.

Apollo was back at Wembley in 1997 as the Saints beat rivals Bradford Bulls once again for their first-ever back-to-back Challenge Cup success. His season was punctuated by injury and he needed operations on both elbows to restore him to full fitness. He continued to be one of the most durable and effective forwards in the British game, however, and in a blockbusting Grand Final against Bradford Bulls in 1999 it was Perelini's surging break that enabled Kevin Iro to score the winning try. He returned to the Theatre of Dreams twelve months later as the Saints repeated their Grand Final success against Wigan – Apollo's swansong as a rugby league player. A two-season spell at Sale Sharks RUFC followed before Apollo returned to Knowsley Road as conditioner, where he remains, highly respected and as popular as ever.

Geoff Pimblett
Full-back 1971-1979

Previous club: St Helens RUFC

St Helens debut: 27 February 1971 v. Whitehaven

Final St Helens appearance: 1 April 1979 v. Wakefield Trinity

Appearances: 360 + 5 subs

Tries: 48

Goals: 608

Drop-goals: 28

Points: 1,388

Transferred to: Retired

Representative honours: Lancashire, England

By the late 1960s, Geoff Pimblett had already made quite an impression in local rugby union circles before he turned professional. He was a centre at St Helens RUFC and captained the side, gaining Lancashire honours in the process. Geoff showed all the attributes that would make him such a brilliant rugby player: nimble feet, a great sidestep, well-timed pass, good kicking game and an astute tactical brain. Yet at twenty-five, he felt that he had gone as far as he could and Saints came in with an offer that he duly accepted, on 7 January 1971.

After several matches in the 'A' team, he made his debut at Whitehaven as a substitute and made his first start against Featherstone Rovers as a stand-off. He wore the full-back's jersey for the first time against Wigan on Good Friday at Central Park, with the Saints winning 9-6. By the end of the campaign, twelve matches in fact, Geoff was playing a vital role in another Saints' success over Wigan, at Swinton in the Championship final, when they kept the trophy for the second successive year.

Geoff had certainly arrived at Knowsley Road at the right time. The next eight seasons were punctuated with finals, winner's medals and Man of the Match awards, as Geoff made the No.1 jersey his own. He was the first player to win both the Lance Todd Trophy (1976 v. Widnes) and Harry Sunderland Trophy (1977 v. Warrington) and led the goal-kicking charts in 1977/78 with 138. He also became the only man to captain both St Helens RUFC and St Helens RLFC.

He made a sterling contribution towards Saints' success in the 1972 Challenge Cup final victory over a powerful Leeds side and was a virtual ever-present in the team that won the First Division Championship in 1975 at a canter. He was, by this time, the principal goal-kicker, addressing the ball in his own distinctive 'nine iron' style. Yet it is the 1976 Challenge Cup final that saw him produce his greatest performance. 'We were playing good rugby that season – the best I had experienced in a Saints' side,' he recalled. 'Once we got the breakthrough, you could enjoy the experience of playing at Wembley.' Despite the intense heat, Pimblett was a constant threat to the Widnes defence all afternoon doing what he did best – linking up with the attack. He also contributed three conversions and two vital drop-goals to the

cause – a superb all-round performance worthy of the coveted Lance Todd Trophy. Following a 15-2 Premiership success against Salford seven days later, Geoff and his teammates embarked on a short tour Down Under, playing against Easts at the Sydney Cricket Ground, but were beaten decisively.

The Saints, with Geoff Pimblett in sparkling form, retained the Premiership trophy in 1977, with the 32-20 defeat of Warrington. Pimblett's marvellous seven goals and a try earned him the Harry Sunderland Trophy outright, not to mention the numerous times he chimed into the three-quarter line with deadly effect. He had also perfected a superb front-on 'man-and-ball' tackle. Not many got past him.

Geoff was the natural choice as club captain following the departures of Billy Benyon and Kel Coslett and he skippered the team in the classic 1978 Challenge Cup final against Leeds. Unfortunately, the heavier Leeds pack triumphed that day, 14-12, in one of the classic Wembley finals.

Already a 'dual-code' county player, Pimblett achieved a long-standing ambition by playing for England against Wales at Knowsley Road on 28 May 1978. England won 60-13, the widest-ever margin between the two countries, yet Geoff delighted his supporters with a fabulous twenty-one-point performance – nine goals – and a try, a record for an England player at the time.

The 1978/79 season saw the Saints in relative decline, although the side battled through to the semi-final of the Challenge Cup against Hull KR. After a string of bad results, the unthinkable happened and Geoff was dropped before the game. The team itself had not been playing well in the run-up and supporters thought that Pimblett had been made a scapegoat, especially when Saints lost 9-7 and he could have made quite a difference. He remembered:

I decided to call it a day after that. I didn't feel bitter, although the feeling of stability I felt had gone. In the mid-seventies I was making perhaps four tackles in a match. Now it was in double figures. I played with the best and I had no intention of putting on a pair of boots again.

Even after his magnificent playing career had come to an end Geoff has maintained his links with the St Helens club. He is the secretary and a founder member of the St Helens' Past Players' Association. A former senior master at Grange Park/Broadway School he is an integral part of the Saints Smart School, helping local primary schools to visit the club. He was also a great club cricketer – arguably the fastest bowler never to play for Lancashire.

Previous club: St Helens Colts

St Helens debut: 17 March 1976 v. Wakefield Trinity

Final St Helens appearance: 17 October 1986 v. Salford

Appearances: 322 + 10 subs

Tries: 78

Goals: 140

Drop-goals: 73

Points: 604

Transferred to: Widnes

Representative honours: Lancashire, England, Great Britain

Injury robbed loose forward Paul Sculthorpe of captaining Great Britain in the Tri-Nations competition in 2005. Yet the last Saints' player to captain his country in an international series was another No.13 – Harry Pinner, who skippered Great Britain in their drawn series against New Zealand twenty years previously. Harry Pinner was a brilliant footballer, with great distribution, tactical kicking and the ability to read a game. By the turn of the 1980s, everything revolved around him as he was a natural choice as skipper during a period of rebuilding at Knowsley Road.

A local product of the Colts system, Harry made his debut during the 1975/76 season and became a first team regular during the following campaign, where he quickly became a focal point for attacking moves, proving himself at the same time to be a sound place-kicker and drop-goal expert. 1977/78 once again saw him at the hub of the Saints' attack, scoring a career-best 20 tries for good measure. He finished the season at Wembley, in the Challenge Cup final against Leeds, when his towering bomb led to Saints' first try from Graham Liptrot. The

heavier Leeds pack triumphed in the end, however, clawing back a ten-point lead to lift the trophy.

For Harry Pinner, the break-up of the great team of the 1970s meant even greater responsibilities on the pitch, as the club relied upon a core of local youngsters to build for the future. Harry really came into his own during 1984/85, when he captained the Saints in a sensational 26-18 Lancashire Cup final victory against Wigan at Central Park, and in the last game of the season – Harry's 300th as a Saint – he was in outstanding form as St Helens lifted the Premiership Trophy at Elland Road against a powerful Hull KR side. Pinner had the Yorkshire defence in such a paddy at one stage that he waltzed through a huge gap for Saints' sixth try in the seventy-second minute – leaving six Rovers' defenders somewhat nonplussed and flat-footed, expecting a pass that never came. His cheeky grin to his teammates afterwards remains one of the most enduring images in Saints' history. Harry accepted not only the Premiership Trophy, but also the Harry Sunderland Trophy after his brilliant Man of the Match performance.

The holder of the most one-point drop-goals in a career (79), Harry won six Great Britain caps, made three appearances for England and was a Lancashire representative on seven occasions. Unfortunately, he fell out of favour with incoming coach Alex Murphy in 1986 and joined Widnes, in exchange for John Fieldhouse. A member of the Saints' Past Players' Hall of Fame, he finished his career with Bradford Northern and coached at Wigan for a spell before concentrating on the licensed trade.

Andrew Platt

Second-row forward 1982-1988

Previous club: Wigan St Patricks ARLFC

St Helens debut: 22 August 1982 v. Leigh

Final St Helens appearance: 8 May 1988 v. Bradford Northern

Appearances: 170 + 15 Subs

Tries: 68

Goals: 0

Drop-goals: 1

Points: 269

Transferred to: Wigan

Representative honours: Lancashire, Great Britain

Born in Billinge, on 9 October 1963, Andy Platt was not the biggest of players and had to run and tackle above his weight. Yet that did not stop him attaining international status with Great Britain as a second-rower and, later in his career, as a front-row forward with the Wigan club. Platt was one of several youngsters signed in the early 1980s as the Saints looked to rebuild the side that had seen so much success over the past few decades. Everything seemed to gel by the 1984/85 campaign, when local lads, such as Platt, Pinner, Round and Ledger, were joined by Australian imports Mal Meninga and Phil Veivers. There was an air of optimism in the town that the team could once again challenge for major honours and Andy Platt was an integral member of the side, famed for his scientific, copy-book tackling and strong running, which brought him no fewer than 19 tries during the campaign. Indeed he scored four touchdowns in a thrilling 30-28 victory against Warrington and followed up with a brace against Wigan in the next match at Central Park, which the Saints won 30-19.

Platt won his first honour with the Saints after a magnificent 26-18 victory against Wigan at Central Park in the Lancashire Cup final. They went on to produce a marvellous performance to beat Hull KR in the Premiership final at Elland Road, Leeds, where Platt's skills were much in evidence. Andy made his Great Britain debut as a substitute on 1 March 1985 against France at Headingley and was selected on the bench against the 1986 Kangaroos in the Second Test at Elland Road, where the visitors enjoyed a 34-4 victory to clinch the rubber. Overall he made four full and three substitute appearances for his country during his St Helens career.

At club level, Platt enjoyed fluctuating fortunes, with defeat in the 1987 Challenge Cup final at the hands of Halifax and a marvellous 15-14 win over Leeds in the John Player Trophy final in the Central Park mud. By this time he was operating as a loose forward and his form was such that he was an automatic selection for the 1988 Great Britain squad for the Australasian tour, together with his Saints' teammates Roy Haggerty, Paul Loughlin and Paul Groves. Andy played in the first two Test matches against Australia, in the second row, although the British were beaten on both occasions.

Much to the disdain of Saints' supporters, he was transferred to Wigan shortly afterwards, where he became a mobile front-rower, gaining multiple honours at club and international level with the Riversiders. He later joined the fledgling Auckland Warriors and finished his career back home with Salford.

Alan Prescott

Front-row forward 1948-1960

Previous club: Halifax

St Helens debut: 15 January 1949 *v.* Belle Vue Rangers

Final St Helens appearance: 19 March 1960 *v.* Halifax

Appearances: 404

Tries: 31

Goals: 0

Points: 93

Transferred to: Retired

Representative honours: Lancashire, England, Great Britain

Alan Prescott was an international rugby league icon, who gained the utmost respect from his on-field deeds and inspirational captaincy. In 1956, Alan was at the pinnacle of his career as captain of his club, county and also his country – the first forward to achieve this particular honour. The Challenge Cup final was a Roses battle royal between St Helens and Halifax – two evenly matched sides. The game was typified by uncompromising tackling, as both sets of forwards vied for supremacy and there was no scoring in a deadlocked first half. After an hour of the match, Alan Prescott embarked upon a surging fifty-yard run through the heart of the Halifax defence. Although his attempted pass to winger Carlton went into touch, it provided a huge psychological boost for his teammates and within minutes the Saints had taken the lead, courtesy of Frank Carlton's scintillating touchdown. Just before the final whistle, Prescott took a gem of a pass from loose forward Vince Karalius to plunge over for a memorable try in the 13-2 success. Alan became the first Saints' captain to lift the cup and was awarded the Lance Todd Trophy into the bargain.

Born in Widnes in 1926, Alan was originally a winger, then loose forward, with Halifax, before becoming a Saint in 1948 for a £2,275 fee. Although he had already played county football as a No.13, he graduated to the front row quite early on in his career at Knowsley Road, on the advice of trainer Peter Lyons. He soon settled into his new role, showing terrific mobility, good hands and was ruthlessly efficient in the tackle. Alan made his international debut against New Zealand in the series-clinching 20-19 victory at Swinton in the Second Test on 10 November 1951 (the first to be televised) and was a permanent fixture in the British team for the next eight years.

The arrival of coach Jim Sullivan galvanised his career at club level, as the Saints went on to lift the Championship in 1952/53 and the Lancashire Cup against Wigan the following year. Prescott skippered the side to their second title success in 1959, after a magnificent spectacle of open football in the clash with Hunslet at a packed Odsal Stadium. Although approaching the end of his playing career, he still showed great mobility and dynamism, at one stage backing up a searing Alex Murphy break in his own twenty-five and feeding Tom van Vollenhoven out wide on the right for his hat-trick try, as the Yorkshiremen were blown away in a magnificent spell in the second half in Saints' 44-22 victory. It is quite clear that with his

inherent pace, Alan would have excelled in the modern-day Super League.

Yet the game for which Alan Prescott is remembered above all is the Second Test at the Brisbane Exhibition Ground on 5 July 1958, when an injury-ravaged Great Britain side overcame unbelievable odds to beat Australia 25-18 and keep the Ashes series alive. Prescott will always be remembered as the Captain Courageous who stayed on the field despite breaking his arm in the fourth minute. Stand-off Dave Bolton had to leave the field with a broken collarbone, yet Challinor, Karalius and Fraser managed to stay on, inspired by the courage of their captain. Twenty-five years later, he recalled the incident vividly:

I tackled Rex Mossop, my arm struck his head and smashed. It went numb and I knew it was broken. I thought to myself, 'You can't go off – this Test Match has got to be won.' I was wondering if I could do any permanent damage, when (Saints' coach) Jim Sullivan's words came back to me - 'if you are only on the field in the way, then someone has to beat you. Always stand and face the opposition, never turn your back.' These words, together with the looks on the

players' faces at Brisbane that day renewed my determination and I knew I had to stay on.

The injury signalled the end of Alan's remarkable twenty-eight Test match career, including two Australian tours (1954 and 1958) and one World Cup campaign (1957). He did not play again for six months, yet his heroic efforts at Brisbane paved the way for a record-breaking 40-17 success for the Lions in the Third Test decider in Sydney. At the end of the match, the team paid a fitting tribute to Prescott's courage by carrying their injured skipper round the ground with the Ashes trophy.

Alan went on to coach St Helens to glory in the 1961 Challenge Cup final against Wigan, but was replaced by Stan McCormick on 16 December 1961 and later coached Leigh for a spell. Although life was difficult for Alan after his playing days finished, he remained an inspirational figure for those who followed. A friendly and extremely articulate man, he passed away on 20 September 1998 aged seventy-one and the St Helens club named a banqueting suite at Knowsley Road in his honour twelve months later. His achievements for the Saints and Great Britain – especially his display of raw courage that day in Brisbane – will never be forgotten.

James 'Butcher' Prescott
Forward 1899-1919

Previous club: Local juniors

St Helens debut: 2 September 1899 v. Warrington

Final St Helens appearance: 4 October 1919 v. Widnes

Appearances: 361

Tries: 70

Goals: 0

Points: 212

Transferred to: Retired

Representative honours: Lancashire

A former pupil of Sacred Heart School in St Helens, James 'Butcher' Prescott was a popular loose forward during the period before the First World War. He was an aggressive player, with great mobility, and a deadly tackler. He cut an impressive figure and became a county representative, only missing out on an Australian tour place because of injury sustained in the trial match – a great shame after such a fine career as a Saint.

The name Butcher came not necessarily from his prowess as a footballer. It was a family name, one borne at times by two of his brothers who played for the Saints before him and were responsible for getting him signed on by the club. It is a great pity that Butcher did not achieve touring status, as he enjoyed much success against Australian teams. He played against the 1909 tourists at Knowsley Road and scored a superb try in the Saints' 9-0 success, when classy centre Harold Greenwood made the opening for him to crash through several visiting defenders. Butcher got on the score-sheet against the Aussies once more, in October 1911. This time he was put through a giant gap by star three-quarter Jimmy Flanagan, but it could not prevent an Australian victory, by 5-16. In the 1911/12 season Butcher scored 16 tries

with his bustling style – a fine achievement for a forward.

James won his first Lancashire cap in the 11-0 defeat by Cumberland on 28 September 1912. Saints' winger Jim Flanagan and scrum-half Fred Trenwith were in the same team. On 29 September 1913, he once again played for Lancashire, against Cumberland in a 24-3 victory at the Cliff, Broughton, and in the 19-11 defeat by Yorkshire at Fartown on 10 December. Both Prescott and teammate Flanagan played in a tour trial at Headingley later in the campaign, but neither was selected.

Butcher became a sergeant in the St Helens Pals during the First World War. One day, at Ypres, he was supervising a trench-cutting operation 'on the top' when a German shell landed close by. He was carried down to the base. One of the stretcher-bearers was club-mate Jimmy Flanagan. Shortly after, Flanagan himself was wounded and the two Pals met again in hospital in England. Butcher was never sent overseas again, but Jimmy went back and paid the ultimate sacrifice. He played one more game for St Helens after the war, before calling it a day.

Butcher then became a 'double agent', as a member of the St Helens Recreation Club Committee – the Saints' big rivals between the wars. Once the Recs had folded in 1939, he still kept an active interest in the game and would regularly attend matches in the north-west for many years.

Austin Rhodes

Scrum-half, full-back 1955-62/1968-69

Previous club: Local juniors

St Helens debut: 28 March 1955 v. Liverpool City

Final St Helens appearance: 19 April 1969 v. Doncaster

Appearances: 265

Tries: 97

Goals: 815

Points: 1870

Transferred to: Leigh (first spell), then retired (second spell)

Representative honours: Lancashire, Great Britain

St Helens won the Challenge Cup for the first time by beating favourites Halifax by 13-2 at Wembley on 28 April 1956. Among the Saints' players who went up to receive their medals that sunny afternoon was a teenage scrum-half called Austin Rhodes who became the first lad from Thatto Heath to win a Challenge Cup winner's medal in a St Helens jersey. The former St Austin's schoolboy star had made his mark with a brilliant long-distance conversion of Steve Llewellyn's try that gave the Saints a commanding 10-0 lead at a vital stage of the match.

An uncompromising footballer, Rhodes played some superb rugby that season which brought him 141 goals and 10 tries in 39 appearances. Always a prodigious points scorer, Saints' fans will remember his typical golfer's approach to goal kicking with his head well over the ball. His excellent club form meant that international football soon beckoned and he was selected for the 1957 British World Cup squad to go to Australia and played against New Zealand to win his first cap.

Although essentially a scrum or stand-off half, Rhodes was converted to full-back after an injury to Glyn Moses and further honours followed with a Championship winner's medal against Hunslet in 1959 and another Challenge Cup winner's medal against the 'old enemy' Wigan in 1961. Once again his kicking at Wembley was instrumental in stretching Saints' winning margin. He punched over two marvellous penalties, one from the

halfway line, to break the hearts of the Wiganers in the 95,000 crowd. Rhodes developed into a fine attacking full-back and was a playing member of the Great Britain World Cup squad in 1960, before winning the last of his four caps against the Kiwis in 1961.

At the end of the 1961/62 season it was time to move on and Austin went to Leigh with teammate Ken Large. A transfer to Swinton followed and it was here that he rediscovered his zest for the game, with the likes of teammates Ken Gowers, John Stopford and Graham Williams.

When former Swinton coach Cliff Evans replaced Joe Coan at Knowsley Road, Austin rejoined his old club, along with Graham Rees for a final fling with the big time. He may not have been as quick as in the early days, but his experience was there for all to see and he picked up another Lancashire Cup winner's medal – his third in all – as St Helens beat Oldham 30-2 in 1968/69. Austin later returned to Swinton as coach for a spell from June 1974 to November 1975. A member of the Saints' Past Players' Hall of Fame, he remains one of the best local footballers the town has ever produced.

Tea Ropati

Stand-off half 1989-1994

Previous club: Mangere East (New Zealand)

St Helens debut: 13 December 1989 v. Dewsbury

Final St Helens appearance: 8 May 1994 v. Wigan

Appearances: 127 + 5 subs

Tries: 56

Goals: 24

Drop-goals: 2

Points: 352

Transferred to: Auckland Warriors (New Zealand)

Representative honours: New Zealand

Big, strong and elusive, with great hands, Tea Ropati was one of several New Zealanders at Knowsley Road during the early 1990s, including skipper Shane Cooper, George Mann and coach Mike McClennan. At 5ft 10ins and just over thirteen stone, he was ideal for the centre or stand-off role and he came with an impressive pedigree. A Kiwi tourist to Australia and Papua New Guinea in 1986, Tea was a member of the Auckland squad who visited Britain twelve months later. He arrived in Britain once more with the Kiwis in 1989, but was restricted to just two matches by injury. Indeed, his initial Saints' career was similarly affected, as he managed just one appearance before he was forced to return to New Zealand.

Once fully fit, his incisive running and silky skills were ideally suited to the Saints' style of fast, open football as the team turned their attentions towards wrestling major honours away from their deadly rivals, Wigan. In 1990/91, the Saints embarked upon a Challenge Cup run that saw them beat highly fancied Widnes in a magnificent semi-final victory only to fall 13-8 at Wembley against the

Riversiders. The 1991/92 campaign saw continued attempts to lift silverware, with Ropati prominent in a 28-16 victory in the Lancashire Cup semi-final victory over Wigan in front of over 17,000 at Knowsley Road. The 24-14 success over Rochdale Hornets, at Wilderspool, provided Tea with his first winner's medal as a Saint, although the team were soundly beaten in the Premiership final by their nemesis at the end of the campaign.

1992/93 was a memorable year for both Tea Ropati and the Saints, as the club vied with Wigan for the Division One Championship, only to lose on points difference. At Old Trafford, however, the Saints won a memorable Premiership final victory over a Wigan outfit looking for an unprecedented Grand Slam, with an influential Ropati in the stand-off role. It was a fine end to the season for Tea, who was named as the Stones Bitter First Division Player of the Year with a record poll of votes. He had been the club's only ever-present with 40 appearances, scoring 141 points including 21 tries. In the Rothman's Rugby League Yearbook Coaches Poll he was a clear winner for the stand-off position for the Coaches' Select XIII ahead of Wigan's Shaun Edwards – no mean feat indeed.

A mild-mannered and amiable character off the field, Tea joined the fledgling Auckland Warriors squad at the end of the 1994/95 season. He came back to Knowsley Road with the Warriors for the inaugural game in the 1997 World Club Championships and overall made seventy-two appearances for the Auckland club. Brothers Joe (Warrington and Swinton), Peter (Leigh) and Iva (Featherstone Rovers) all played in England at some stage.

Paul Sculthorpe

Loose forward 1998-

Previous club: Warrington Wolves

St Helens debut: 15 February 1998 v. Featherstone Rovers

Appearances: 214 +1 sub

Tries: 103

Goals: 333

Drop-goals: 10

Points: 1088

Transferred to:

Representative honours: Lancashire, England, Great Britain

In retrospect, the Saints got a real bargain when they signed Paul Sculthorpe from Warrington on 1 January 1998, despite the fact that he cost a world record fee for a forward of £375,000. By the Millennium, Oldham-born Sculthorpe had developed into one of the most complete players in rugby league. Naturally strong and powerful, with a high level of fitness, he proved his versatility when it was needed at club and international level. Essentially a loose forward, injuries to regular half-backs Sean Long and Tommy Martyn saw Paul switch to stand-off, which he did with great aplomb during the 2001 season. At this time, he also took on the goal-kicking role with great success. Indeed, Paul could play a variety of roles within the team, from a hard-running and tackling back-row forward, to a more creative role with some brilliantly timed passes for his centres. His kicking game consisted of 'downtown' long-range clearances, tantalising grubbers and drop-goals, characterised by his vital one-pointer in the 2001 World Club Championship victory over Brisbane Broncos in 2001.

The team was reconstructed around the midfield trio of Sculthorpe, Long and Cunningham in 1998, with these players being the key to success in the new Millennium. Under coach Ellery Hanley, Paul made thirty-one appearances in the 1999 season, showing superb running and tackling power, climaxed by the team's 8-6 success over Bradford Bulls in the Grand Final at Old Trafford. Sculthorpe remained in the pack for the 2000 campaign, as coach Ian Millward adopted a more entertaining, rather than pragmatic approach. Paul was by now in top form, as the team retained their Super League crown in a 29-16 victory over Wigan.

Paul really came into his own in 2001, winning the Tetley's Super League Man of Steel award; such was the quality of his performances. He played 31 matches for St Helens, scoring 273 points – 27 tries 82 goals and one drop-goal, the latter against Brisbane at the Reebok Stadium. Paul also notched two hat-tricks, against Warrington and Leeds. The World Champions then tackled Bradford Bulls off the park at Twickenham in the Challenge Cup final, with Sculthorpe once more having a pivotal role with another all-action display. As the injuries kicked in, he was a tower of strength, although the team could not repeat their Grand Final success of the previous year. At the season's end, Scully was in outstanding form for Great Britain in the stand-off role, scoring two tries and two drop-goals against

Australia in the First Test, at Huddersfield, as the Kangaroos slumped to a 20-12 defeat. Although Great Britain lost the series, Paul was one of the outstanding performers and would not appear out of place in any NRL line-up Down Under.

Paul's marvellous form continued into 2002, with a Grand Final victory over Bradford Bulls at Old Trafford. Once again, the midfield trio of Sculthorpe, Long and Cunningham dominated for large spells in the second half. Scully's own contributions throughout the campaign were immense – 33 appearances, 17 tries and 114 goals, including ten-goal performances against Hull and Warrington – which once again earned him the prestigious Man of Steel award; the first time that this honour had been won by a player in successive seasons.

Niggling injuries characterised Paul's 2003 campaign, although he was back to his best the following year as captain of the side, when the Saints produced some of the greatest rugby ever witnessed at Knowsley Road, especially in the Challenge Cup, where they reached the final by playing Super League opposition throughout, beginning at Bradford (10-30), then at home to Leeds (24-14), Hull (31-26) and smashed hapless Huddersfield 46-6 at Warrington in the semi-final. Paul, with his younger brother Danny in opposition for Wigan, produced another superb display in the final at the Millennium Stadium, including a fine

short-range score in the fiftieth minute that sealed a marvellous 32-16 success. Off the field, Paul had also become the public face of rugby league for Gillette; only the second British sports star after David Beckham to represent the company.

At the end of 2004, Paul was on international duty once more with Great Britain in the Tri-Nations competition, although they lost out to Australia in the final at Elland Road. There were changes at the helm at Knowsley Road in 2005, with Daniel Anderson replacing Ian Millward as coach. The team went out at the semi-final stage of the Challenge Cup to Hull, although in the longer term, the League Leader's Shield was the reward for consistency, after Leeds looked odds on to secure top spot. Paul registered his 200th appearance for the club, at home to Widnes Vikings on 11 February 2005, yet he played in just sixteen matches during the campaign. Ironically, a serious knee injury wrecked his chances of skippering St Helens in the end of season play-offs and Great Britain, in the Tri-Nations competition. The man who won three Grand Finals, two Challenge Cups and a World Club Championship faced a long off-season in the fight to regain full fitness – hopefully a temporary set-back, before continuing to add to his terrific record of achievement at club and international level. Truly a St Helens all-time great.

Nat Silcock

Second-row, front-row forward 1955-58

Previous club: Wigan

St Helens debut: 22 January 1955 v. Wakefield Trinity

Final St Helens appearance: 30 August 1958 v. Rochdale Hornets

Appearances: 138

Tries: 29

Goals: 0

Points: 87

Transferred to: Warrington

Representative honours: Lancashire

Born in Widnes, and a product of the famous West Bank amateur club, Nat Douglas Silcock followed his father as a Great Britain international and Australian tourist. Unlike his father, however, it was not for his home-town team! Young Nat signed for Wigan and, although essentially a forward, he came to prominence by scoring a try for the Riversiders in the 1950 Championship final on the wing. Nat played nineteen matches on the 1954 Australian tour, including three Test matches against Australia, which the British lost 2-1. He won every major honour with the Cherry and Whites, making 194 appearances and 64 tries before he asked for a transfer at the start of the 1954/55 campaign. After a somewhat drawn-out saga, he was signed by his former coach, Jim Sullivan, to reinforce the strength of the pack at St Helens. At 6ft 1in and just over sixteen stone, he was the biggest forward when he signed for the club. Utilised as a supremely fast and mobile second-rower, he made his debut at Knowsley Road in a convincing 39-7 victory against Wakefield Trinity in January 1955.

His finest moment in the famous red and white of St Helens was at Wembley in the 1956 Challenge Cup final, when his ferocious running out wide did much to soften up the Halifax defence in what was, essentially, a game of attrition. With his inherent mobility, Nat would have been very much at home in modern-day Super League. Saints' legend Duggie Greenall, who had toured with him in 1954, rated Nat very highly indeed:

He became the star forward at Knowsley Road when he joined us. He was a great player with a good football brain, very fast and a brilliant tackler. If I was picking my greatest-ever team, he would be in my second row. Nat never shirked anything on the field!

A brick-layer by trade, who also spent time down the pit, Nat went on to play in the Lancashire Cup final on 20 October 1956, when the Saints were defeated 10-3 by a powerful Oldham outfit. Although Silcock did not make any further appearances for his country, he was a member of the Lancashire team that won the County Championship in 1956/57, with wins against Cumberland and Yorkshire – the latter a terrific 35-21 success at Hull.

At the start of the 1959/59 season, however, Nat was transferred to Warrington and, operating as an open-side prop, played against St Helens in the 1959 Lancashire Cup final resulting in a 5-4 success! In May 1961 at the latter end of his career, he emigrated to Australia and played in the Newcastle competition before joining Eastern Suburbs in Sydney and captaining the team for a spell. On returning home some years later, he ran the Blackburn Arms and Railway Hotel in Warrington.

Wilf Smith
Scrum-half, stand-off 1955-1969

Previous club: Clock Face ARLFC

St Helens debut: 12 November 1955 v. Halifax

Final St Helens appearance: 4 April 1969 v. Wigan

Appearances: 195 + 5 subs

Tries: 55

Goals: 1

Points: 167

Transferred to: Retired

Representative honours: None

Wilf was a stalwart of the St Helens club for fourteen years, winning virtually every honour in the game during his career at Knowsley Road. Rugby league was in his blood – his father, Tommy, was a fine second-row forward with the mighty St Helens Recs in the 1920s and part of the famous 'Smith, Fildes and Mulvanney' back three. A great all-round footballer, with good hands and a clinical tackler, he signed for the Saints from the Clock Face amateur club on 15 September 1955 and learned his trade in the 'A' team before emerging as a stand-off outside the legendary scrum-half Alex Murphy in 1958/59, a season when the Saints won the Championship final after an epic 44-22 victory over Hunslet. Wilf scored a magical try in the second half, slicing through the opposition defence in a thirty-yard run to the line.

The Smith-Murphy combination at half-back was once again seen at its best at Wembley in 1961, when the Saints beat deadly rivals Wigan 12-6 in the baking sun. Wilf's prodigious work-rate and solid defence were one of the features of his team's success. He appeared in three more Championship finals, in 1965, when the Saints lost to a powerful Halifax side at Swinton and two years later, when Wakefield Trinity lifted the silverware after a replay

at the same venue, in front of 33,000 spectators. Wilf played in every position in the backs for Saints during his career and never gave anything less than 100 per cent. It was indeed a pity that such a fine player never achieved county recognition, but competition in those days was tough.

Wilf played just fifteen matches in Saints' four cups season in 1965/66, as a result of a persistent knee injury, although he appeared in five Lancashire Cup finals for the club, winning four, against Swinton (1961 and 1962), Leigh (1963), when he played left centre, and scored a memorable try and in the replayed final against Warrington in 1967, when he was centre to the great Tom van Vollenhoven. His much-needed experience in the back line was a major contribution to Saints' 13-10 success. All told, he played in ten major finals for the club, including replays – a fantastic achievement. He will always be remembered as a solid, reliable footballer and he was awarded a well-earned benefit in the 1967/68 season.

Wilf took up a coaching position with Blackpool Borough and became assistant coach at Wigan, with George Fairburn and Maurice Bamford in the early 1980s, before becoming involved with the amateur game at Blackbrook and Bold. He remains knowledgeable and enthusiastic about the modern game and is a popular member of the St Helens' Past Players' Hall of Fame

Previous club: United Glass Bottle Manufacturers ARLFC

St Helens debut: 4 November 1939 v. Broughton Rangers

Final St Helens appearance: 22 November 1952 v. Warrington

Appearances: 193

Tries: 65

Goals: 295

Points: 785

Transferred to: Retired

Representative honours: Lancashire, England, Great Britain

Saints' captain and their most influential attacking player during the early post-war years was Jimmy Stott, a local lad from Parr. He was a good all-round sportsman who played soccer at fourteen for Lancashire Schoolboys – Tommy Lawton was in the same team. Jimmy continued to play soccer for his employers, UGB, as a seventeen-year-old, but turned out one day for the rugby team when they were a man short and became converted to the thirteen-a-side code. It was playing for UGB against Hunslet in the first round of the Challenge Cup in 1939 that he was first spotted, and despite offers from Wigan, Halifax and Hunslet, Jimmy signed for his home-town team.

In February 1940 he joined the army and remained in the forces for six years. If Stott had been in club football during that time he would have been the best centre of his generation. He had so much ability to play attacking football – change of pace, sidestep, convincing dummy, perfectly judged punt, drop-kick in either foot – but not the opportunity to show his talents at their best. An army rugby union representative, Craftsman J. Stott did, however, play for a rugby league XV against a rugby union XV, at Odsal Stadium, in 1944, under rugby union rules for Service Charities. The score – 15-10 to the league lads.

In a League match at Station Road, Swinton in April 1947 his match-winning qualities were shown to great effect when he notched a hat-trick of tries. The third try in particular was a real beauty,

just when Swinton were getting back into the game. One critic described it as: 'A dancing master's exposition of the pirouette, a dodging slow and fast spurting hand-bluffing piece of wizardry.' This was typical Jimmy Stott. The home defenders expected him to pass all the time but he never did.

Jimmy captained the Saints during the difficult period following the end of the Second World War, when the club was rebuilding its playing strength. He made his one and only appearance in the Great Britain side for the First Test match against Leeds on 4 October 1947, together with his Saints' teammate Len Aston. This was ample compensation for the man who might well have toured Down Under in 1946, but for a late demob. A county representative, he also played twice for England in 1946/47.

Jimmy felt that a lot of enjoyment has gone out of the modern game. 'I played for the love of it, and if a fellow was better than me on the day, the best of luck to him.' Typical Jimmy Stott, a man who played the game for the game's sake. A great crowd favourite and a real gentleman, he was rewarded with a benefit in 1950. Jim Stott died on 6 July 1994.

Anthony Sullivan
Winger 1991-2001

Previous club: Hull KR

St Helens debut: 1 September 1991 v. Hull

Final St Helens appearance: 17 August 2001 v. Bradford Bulls

Appearances: 298 + 7 subs

Tries: 213

Goals: 5

Points: 862

Transferred to: Cardiff RUFC

Representative honours: Yorkshire, Wales, Great Britain

Anthony Sullivan was a real flying machine on the left wing for the Saints – and Wales – during his ten years at Knowsley Road. His try-scoring feats are legendary, including his finest moment, against Wigan at the JJB during the Super League qualifying semi-final in 2000. The Saints were 12-6 up just before half-time when Wigan scrum-half Peters hoisted a towering bomb from halfway towards the right-hand touchline, where it was caught by Sullivan, just outside the twenty metre line. Sully brushed off the first challenge from his opposite number Dallas and set off along the touchline, with centre Gary Connolly in hot pursuit. As Connolly made one despairing lunge, Sully suddenly switched to the inside, totally wrong-footing Radlinski and Jason Robinson, before diving over the line – a magnificent piece of balanced running at pace. Saints went on to win 54-16 and clinch a Grand Final spot at Old Trafford – where Anthony Sullivan and his teammates beat Wigan once more to lift the trophy.

Anthony was born into a rugby league dynasty on 23 November 1968. His father was the great Clive Sullivan, who had played with distinction for both Hull clubs and captained Great Britain to World Cup glory in 1972. Although initially a soccer player, Anthony turned to rugby league with Hull KR and was signed by the Saints for £80,000 on 29 April 1991. He was a member of a potent three-quarter line, yet he struggled to find consistency in his first few years at Knowsley Road, despite a Lancashire Cup winner's medal in 1991.

It was only after the advent of the European Super League in 1996 that Anthony showed just how good a winger he was, revelling on the harder grounds of summer. He also had a great centre partner – Paul Newlove – making them one of the most feared combinations in the League. Sully finished with 23 tries from 22 appearances and was included in the Coaches' Select XIII – a season in which the Saints had finished top of the inaugural Super League competition and defeated Bradford Bulls in their first Wembley success for twenty years. Sully scored a try in a repeat performance against the Bulls twelve months later, latching on to a raking Tommy Martyn grubber and success continued unabated. He appeared in one more Challenge Cup final, against Bradford at Twickenham in 2001, two Grand Finals (1999 and 2000) and a World Club Championship clash against Brisbane at Bolton in 2001 – winning them all.

A thoughtful and articulate man, Sully represented Wales with great pride and became a dual international, with three appearances for the Welsh rugby union 'A' side in 1999, during a short spell with Cardiff RUFC. After a well-earned testimonial at Knowsley Road, Sully re-joined Cardiff in 2001 on a two-year contract, before retiring. His status among the great wingers in Saints' history is assured.

Mick Sullivan
Winger 1961-1963

Previous club: Wigan

St Helens debut: 16 January 1961 v. Hull

Final St Helens appearance: 30 May 1963 v. Oldham

Appearances: 82

Tries: 31

Goals: 0

Points: 93

Transferred to: York

Representative honours: Yorkshire, Great Britain

One of the greatest post-war left wingers, Pudsey-born Mick Sullivan holds two incredible records in Test match football. The former Shaw Cross junior made 46 appearances for Great Britain – 16 against Australia, 11 against New Zealand and 19 against France – which included a remarkable run of 36 successive matches. Fast and skilful in attack, extremely robust in defence, he scored another record 38 tries in 19 matches during the second of his three tours to Australia, in 1958.

Mick made his name in the 1954 World Cup in France and wore an international jersey each year between 1954 and 1963 – a phenomenal achievement – during which time he played for four different clubs. He began at Huddersfield and was bought by Wigan for a then record £9,500 fee in 1957. Sully won two Challenge Cup winner's medals with the Riversiders in 1958 and 1959, scoring a try in both matches.

Mick was signed by Harry Cook before the 1961 Challenge Cup deadline, for another world record fee of £11,500. Sullivan made his debut for Saints on 16 January 1961 in the centre, scoring a try in a hard fought 22-15 victory over Hull at Knowsley Road. He scored 4 tries in 19 matches during the season, which ended with him facing his former Wigan teammates at Wembley – and Billy Boston in particular – where he picked up his third winner's medal. There were times when Sully's experience was utilised both at centre and stand-off, when he was required to mark a potentially dangerous

opponent out of the game. Although barely twelve stone, he was renowned for his tackling ability. Yet he could still fly down the touchline, once scoring five tries in a League match against Huddersfield at Knowsley Road in 1963. Mick won two Lancashire Cup winner's medals with the Saints in 1961/62 and 1962/63 and continued his impressive record in representative football, gaining ten Great Britain caps and playing three times for Yorkshire in the County Championship.

Sully went on to join York for £2,000 in 1963. He left the Minstermen a few years later to become player-coach at Dewsbury and as a loose forward led them to the semi-final of the Challenge Cup only to be beaten 12-5 by his old club St Helens, who went on to lift the trophy.

Sully then went to Australia to play club football and, at the request of the Australian League, he was suspended for joining the rebel League club Junee. Although this was later lifted, it was here that he received his most serious injury of his career, breaking his jaw in seven places. He eventually returned to England and had a spell as coach to Bradford and Batley before leaving the game in the early 1970s. He was a prison officer at Wakefield for many years.

Albert Terry

Previous club: Local juniors

St Helens debut: 18 April 1955 v. Barrow

Final St Helens appearance: 2 December 1961 v. Hull KR

Appearances: 216

Tries: 27

Goals: 0

Points: 81

Transferred to: Leeds

Representative honours: Lancashire, Great Britain

Born in St Helens on 17 May 1934, Albert Edward Terry was a superb front-row forward, who came through the ranks at Knowsley Road, first coming to prominence against the Australian touring side in 1956 when the Saints inflicted a record defeat on the tourists by 44 points to 2. All members of the pack scored that day against the famous 'Green and Golds', an unusual occurrence indeed.

It was no surprise when the twenty-three-year-old Terry was selected for the 1958 Australian tour, along with five of his teammates – Alex Murphy, Glyn Moses, Vince Karalius, Frank Carlton and captain Alan Prescott. Great Britain lost the First Test 25-8, in Sydney, where Terry made his Test debut. He was replaced by Brian McTigue in the Second Test at Brisbane, but was recalled for the Third Test, at Sydney once more. It was a superb performance from Great Britain, who trounced the Aussies 40-17! Great Britain's second try, in the twenty-second minute, was a real belter. The Australian defence was taking a real battering when Huddart off-loaded to Terry, some forty metres from the Australian's line. Abe saw a gap open up before him and put his foot down, getting into some open space. As the cover regrouped, he stepped inside, in full stride, beat one defender for sheer pace and bumped off full-back Clifford, before diving over under the sticks in grand style. Terry went on to play in all the matches when the Kangaroos toured in 1959, when Britain retained the Ashes. He played in eleven Tests overall, his last against the French, at Leeds in 1962. He also represented Lancashire on two occasions.

Abe returned to St Helens after the 1958 tour to become part of a formidable pack, strengthened by the acquisition of his touring colleague Dick Huddart, from Whitehaven. The side broke all records, scoring over 1,000 points and lifting the coveted championship trophy after a sensational 44-22 success over Hunslet, at Odsal Stadium, Bradford.

The 1960/61 season was another great one for the Saints. A young Cliff Watson had replaced Alan Prescott in the front row, with Bob Dagnall coming in as hooker. Abe was, once again, the cornerstone of the pack as the team defeated Swinton 15-9 at Central Park, Wigan, to win the Lancashire Cup and then, the climax to the season – a wonderful 12-6 victory over Wigan in one of the hottest finals ever played at Wembley. Abe's Saints' career was to end, rather disappointingly, when he was sold to Leeds in December 1961 for £8,000 – one of several established players to leave the club at the time. He had further spells with Featherstone and Castleford, before retirement. Abe's brother, Fred, also played with him in the same Saints' team on twenty-five occasions, before his transfer to Blackpool Borough. Abe is a worthy member of the Saints' Past Players' Hall of Fame.

Hubert 'Jum' Turtill

Full-back 1909-1914

Previous club: Canterbury (New Zealand)

St Helens debut: 2 September 1909 v. Hull KR

Final St Helens appearance: 21 February 1914 v. Warrington

Appearances: 137

Tries: 3

Goals: 197

Points: 403

Transferred to: Retired

Representative honours: New Zealand

The pioneering New Zealand tourists from 1907/08 held a special affection for St Helens, as it was the birthplace of their first Prime Minister, Richard Seddon. This was a major reason why the Saints, arguably one of the league's poorer relations at the time, were able to secure the services of HS Turtill for the start of the 1909/10 season. He had gained a fearsome reputation on the tour and in the opinion of many who saw him he was the world's best full-back. He could kick well with either foot, and was gifted with tremendous tackling power and a fine turn of speed.

Hubert Sydney Turtill was born in London, but as an infant went to New Zealand with his parents in 1884. A chubby youngster who was nicknamed 'Jumbo' by the passengers travelling with his family on the ship out and later shortened to 'Jum' – the name that remained with him for the rest of his life. He later returned to England with his wife, who was New Zealand-born, to sign for Salford, but he joined St Helens instead for a £150 fee. Turtill's friend on tour, Arthur Kelly had become Saints' first-ever overseas signing shortly before – a big influence on his decision.

His signing was the talk of the Northern Union and he became an ever-present in his first season at Knowsley Road. He added a whole new dimension to full-back play with his adventurous attacking instincts. Jum became the first player in the club's history to kick fifty goals and score a century of points, which he achieved in his first season with the Saints. His best return for the club was 61 goals in 1911/12. He opened a tobacconists shop in Duke Street and when the new Saints' jersey of blue and black hoops was displayed in the window, the police had to move the crowds along.

A tremendously popular fellow with the supporters, Jum became mine host of the Nelson Hotel and, in September 1914, he became the first publican in the town to answer his country's call when he joined the St Helens Engineers. Four years later, it was to end in tragedy and he became another statistic of the grim conflict on the Western Front, when he was killed in his billet by shrapnel on the morning of 9 April 1918. A letter of condolence from the battlefield to his wife was written by his Company Quarter Master Sergeant, Harry Mercer – the former Saints' secretary.

Jum Turtill was the Saints' first big-name overseas signing and did much to elevate the status of the St Helens club in the years just before 1914. Sadly, Jum's son Alan was also a victim of the Second World War and his name can be seen on the War Memorial in Victoria Square.

Tom van Vollenhoven
Winger 1957-1968

Previous club: Northern Transvaal RU (South Africa)

St Helens debut: 26 October 1957 v. Leeds

Final St Helens appearance: 27 April 1968 v. Hull KR

Appearances: 408

Tries: 392

Goals: 0

Points: 1,176

Transferred to: Retired

Representative honours: Other Nationalities

'The greatest of them all,' say the lyrics to the Vollenhoven Calypso – a seven inch record released to coincide with his testimonial season in 1967/68. It has always been a matter of debate as to whether the flying Springbok was, actually, the best winger of his generation in English rugby league. Wigan fans point to the block-busting ability of Billy Boston, while over at Wilderspool, Brian Bevan was breaking all try-scoring records with his particularly unorthodox – some would say freakish – attacking style. Yet Tom van Vollenhoven is without question the greatest winger to wear the famous red and white jersey, although, once again, Alf Ellaby, a star of the late 1920s, is also championed by a host of Knowsley Road greybeards.

Tommy Vol was truly a phenomenon, with 392 tries in 408 appearances – says it all, doesn't it? A blond, crew-cutted figure, who possessed terrific pace and athletic ability, he was also extremely strong for his size. Tom would finish with aplomb if given only minimal space down the touchline. He could conjure up tries from the most unlikely scenarios, regardless of the craft and skill of his centres. Former Liverpool City full-back Ray Ashby came up with this engaging tribute, after he tried in vain to stop the great man from scoring: 'I got hold of him – and he just disappeared!'

Those who witnessed his incredible three-try performance against Hunslet in the 1959 Championship final at Odsal could scarcely believe what they were seeing. Until Tom's intervention, there was a real chance that the Yorkshiremen would have snatched the initiative – and he notched up his hat-trick despite the pain of a torn hamstring, that took most of the summer to heal. What he would have been like fully fit is anybody's guess.

He was nursed in gently in his early days at Knowsley Road by legendary centre Duggie Greenall, although his most famous touchdown involved superb interplay with another fine three-quarter, Ken Large, at Wembley in the 1961 Challenge Cup final against Wigan. He played in two Wembley finals, both against the 'old enemy', with Saints lifting the coveted trophy each time.

Tom was also a superb defensive wingman, rushing over to the other flank to pull off many

a try-saving tackle. It is this aspect of his game that certainly took him past Ellaby, who was not particularly renowned for his defensive qualities. He was, however, first and foremost a winger. He had spells at centre and even one game at full-back, but it didn't suit. Inevitably, injury took its toll by the mid-1960s. His opponents would do anything to stop him, such as the ferocious stiff-arm unleashed by Huddersfield's Peter Ramsden during a particularly ill-tempered Challenge Cup tie at Knowsley Road in 1963, which left Vol lying prostrate on the turf like a spent balloon. Despite the heavy tackles, it was never in Tom's nature to retaliate and he remained a true sportsman to the end.

He was reduced to the status of a 'very good' club class winger during his final season in 1967/68, although he was still capable of notching three tries in his last derby match appearance against Wigan at Knowsley Road. The £2,800 testimonial cheque he received at the end of June 1968 was a rugby league record. In presenting it, Harry Cook called him the greatest-ever winger. Few will argue – there will never be another 'Van'. His final game of rugby league was guesting for Great Britain in a trial match for the 1968 World Cup, at Thrum Hall, Halifax.

Back in 1957, the 'Vollenhoven Effect' was immediate, with Tom scoring on his debut against Leeds at Knowsley Road and he was able to add much-needed 'pep' to a side that had previously been under criticism for its negative, forward-orientated football. Of course, all that was soon to change. The Saints went on to produce one of the great displays of attacking football in the 1959 Championship final, with fellow South African Jan Prinsloo on the other flank. His signing, a top-secret affair from under the noses of the South African rugby union authorities, and under intense competition from Wigan, is a story in itself and cost the club £7,230 – the biggest fee paid for a rugby union player or for a transfer between professional clubs, but it was money well spent. I'm sure that even the astute Saints' chairman Harry Cook could not have really foreseen what an effect this fellow would have on the team and the town. It was always a nervous time if Tom went home for the summer. We were only really happy once he returned. He was the obvious choice to front the club's centenary celebrations in 1990 and spent almost three hours the day before signing up to 500 autographs at the Saints' Exhibition at the town's museum in College Street. Fans queued around the block to meet him. You were left in no doubt what he will always mean to the people of St Helens – a genuine superstar. Tom was inducted into rugby league's Hall of Fame in 2000; further proof of his status in the greatest game.

Phil Veivers
Full-back, centre 1984-1996

Previous club: Brisbane Souths (Australia)

St Helens debut: 7 October 1984 v. Castleford

Final St Helens appearance: 31 March 1996 v. Workington Town

Appearances: 332 + 49 subs

Tries: 98

Goals: 0

Drop-goals: 5

Points: 397

Transferred to: Huddersfield Giants

Representative honours: None

P hil Veivers is a genuine Knowsley Road legend. His family is steeped in rugby league history – his cousin, Mick, and brother, Greg, both played for Australia and his brother-in-law is Australia's longest-serving First Grade coach, Wayne Bennett, of the Brisbane Broncos. Born in Beaudesert, Queensland, on 25 May 1964, Phil began his career at the famous Brisbane Souths club, before the offer came of a move to St Helens, as part of the Mal Meninga deal. He originally only planned to stay for twelve months, yet he ended up being offered a three-year contract by the Saints – and has stayed in the 'Old Dart' ever since.

Phil became an instant success as a full-back, who brought a new dimension to the British game; soaring high to pluck dangerous 'bombs' out of the air with contemptuous ease. He had excellent handling skills, possessed a spectacular 'diving' tackling technique and knew instinctively when to join the three-quarter line. Phil had a brilliant first season at Knowsley Road, as the young Saints' side – galvanised by the presence of Meninga – went on to lift the Lancashire Cup against Wigan and finished the season in grand style with a storming 36-16 victory in the Premiership final against a powerful Hull KR side, when Veivers notched a typically opportunist touchdown.

Although the Saints could always be relied upon to play fast, entertaining rugby during Phil's career, they were very often bridesmaids at the expense of a full-time Wigan outfit and he suffered two Challenge Cup final reversals at the hands of the Riversiders in 1989 and 1991. Yet Veivers showed just what a class act he was, as favourites Widnes were beaten by the unfancied Saints in both semi-finals. Phil also tasted defeat in the 1987 final against Halifax, a match that St Helens should really have won comfortably.

Despite the disappointments of Wembley, Veivers was a vital cog in the Saints' attacking machine of the late 1980s and early '90s, together with other overseas signings such as Shane Cooper – with whom he had a brilliant understanding – Tea Ropati and George Mann. He excelled in the mud of Central Park as Saints defeated a strong Leeds side in their John Player Trophy success in 1988 and scored two superb tries at stand off during Saints' 24-14 Lancashire Cup success over Rochdale Hornets in 1991. He spent part of his final years at Knowsley Road as a utility player, excelling in the acting half-back role. He enjoyed a well-deserved testimonial at St Helens and made just one appearance in the new Super League competition before his transfer to Huddersfield, where he took on a player-coach role. Veivers captained Huddersfield to victory in the 1997 Divisional Premiership final against Hull Sharks and by the 2005 Super League campaign was assistant coach to Brian Noble at Bradford Bulls. He was a fantastic natural footballer – a real Saints' great.

Previous club: Local juniors

St Helens debut: 15 April 1968 v. Swinton

Final St Helens appearance: 17 May 1975 v. Leeds

Appearances: 181 + 4 subs

Tries: 48

Goals: 156

Points: 456

Transferred to: Retired

Representative honours: Lancashire, England, Great Britain

A former pupil at Grange Park Technical School in St Helens, who went on to further education at Hull University, John Walsh was a brilliant all-round sportsman, who played rugby union at the local St Helens club, before joining a newly formed rugby league team at Moss Bank. The club won the Lancashire Cup in its first season and in 1968 John was selected to tour Australia with the GB Amateur RL team. At the same time, Saints stepped in to sign him and he was soon making his debut on 15 April 1968 at Swinton, where he kicked two goals in Saints' 19-16 success.

Despite the presence of Austin Rhodes and Frank Barrow, John made seventeen appearances at full-back in 1968/69 and his 'round-the-corner' kicking style, unusual at the time, brought him 27 goals. He was a first team regular during the next season, operating in both centre and full-back berths. Yet it was as a centre that he was most effective, where he was able to send his winger Frank Wilson in for a host of touchdowns. The team reached the Championship final against Leeds, at Odsal where John had a storming game, troubling the Leeds' backs constantly with his probing runs and crunching one-on-one tackles – scoring a try and two goals for good measure.

Saints retained the Championship the following season with a remarkable 16-12 success over rivals Wigan at Station Road, Swinton. Walsh's attempted drop-goal was seized upon by Billy Benyon, who crashed over the line to complete an unlikely victory almost on the final whistle. John continued to be prominent in Saints' success,

with a devastating performance in a 17-0 defeat of Leeds at Headingley in the BBC2 Floodlit Trophy semi-final. Leeds were again victims in the Challenge Cup final of 1972, when a fabulous defensive display by Walsh snuffed out the threat of Leeds' Syd Hynes. A Lancashire county representative, he reached the pinnacle of his career, playing centre in the Great Britain team that became World Champions in the tournament held in France. In a tense final in Lyons, Great Britain and Australia drew 10-10 after extra time, but the tournament was awarded to the British, who had more points from the group games.

Walsh played in barely half of Saints' matches in 1972/73 and he took a sabbatical the following season to concentrate on his examinations; a decision that cost him a place on the 1974 Lions tour. He was back to his best in 1974/75 however, as the Saints clinched the First Division Championship, losing just three matches in the process. He played in two matches in the 1975 World Championships for England, before announcing his retirement, just before his twenty-ninth birthday. One of the best footballers of his generation, John later settled in Canada, where he was able to pursue his career as an actuary.

Kevin Ward
Front-row forward 1990-1993

Previous club: Castleford

St Helens debut: 26 August 1990 v. Trafford Borough

Final St Helens appearance: 9 April 1993 v. Wigan

Appearances: 86 + 3 subs

Tries: 8

Goals: 0

Points: 32

Transferred to: Retired

Representative honours: Great Britain

A true giant amongst men, Kevin Ward joined the Saints from Castleford in July 1990 and made eighty-six appearances for the club in three seasons at Knowsley Road. Kevin won virtually every honour in the game with his three clubs – Castleford, St Helens and Manly (Australia) – yet his career came to an abrupt end playing for St Helens against Wigan at Central Park on Good Friday 1993. His shattered left ankle and lower leg meant a nightmare two years of painfully slow recovery and, at one stage, it looked as though amputation was the only option. His leg will never be the same again, yet Kevin's display of courage in adversity is so typical of the man. Although the Saints' Division One title hopes virtually disappeared that day in an 8-8 draw, Wardy's teammates used it as a spur to beat those same opponents in the Premiership final at Old Trafford, in a memorable 10-4 success. Needless to say, Kevin joined the team on the pitch on his crutches, yet nobody realised the prolonged fitness battle that lay ahead.

Born in Stanley, West Yorkshire on 5 August 1957, Kevin was thirty-three years old when he signed for Saints for an £80,000 fee. His sheer presence brought out the best from players around him, such as fellow props Jon Neill, John Harrison and New Zealander George Mann. Indeed Kevin produced an inspirational performance in the 1991 Challenge Cup semi-final against Widnes at Central Park, where his bursts down the centre of the field and timely off-loads caused absolute mayhem. Supremely strong, with great stamina, Kevin had a prodigious appetite for work. He was an eighty-minute player who hated being subbed, and was the archetypal pack enforcer, reminiscent of the great Cliff Watson, another master of the art of front-row play.

Kevin signed for Castleford from Stanley Rangers and made his debut in 1979, making 304 appearances for the Wheldon Road club, winning his first honour for the Great Britain Under-24 side the following year. He played in five Yorkshire Cups, winning two, and helped Castleford to victory at Wembley in 1986. Kevin also had a spell with the Manly club, helping them to an 18-8 Grand Final success against Canberra on 27 September 1987. A seasoned international footballer, with fifteen Test caps, and an Australian tourist in 1988, Kevin appeared in the 1992 World Cup final as a result of his superb form for the Saints. He played in the 1991 Challenge Cup final defeat by Wigan and added a Lancashire Cup winner's medal to his collection after St Helens beat Rochdale Hornets in 1991/92. He remains a legendary figure at Knowsley Road and is recognised as one of the greatest front-row forwards of all time, revered in both the UK and Australia.

John Warlow

Second-row, front-row forward 1963-70/1973-1975

Previous club: Llanelli RUFC (Wales)

St Helens debut: 30 November 1963 v. Liverpool City

Final St Helens appearance: 17 May 1975 v. Leeds

Appearances: 235 + 10 subs

Tries: 27

Goals: 0

Points: 81

Transferred to: Widnes (first spell), Rochdale Hornets (second spell)

Representative honours: Wales, Great Britain

Born in Llanelli on 13 February 1939, 'Big John' Warlow played for Llanelli and made one international appearance for Wales before the Saints showed an interest. He was signed in a local public house by chairman Harry Cook and secretary Basil Lowe on 23 October 1963, with directors from Workington Town also intent on getting their man. Harry Cook's persuasive manner did the trick, however, and Warlow was able to celebrate his switch of codes with most of his former teammates.

At over 6ft in height and weighing more than fifteen stone, John was an uncompromising forward – a real tough nut with the ball in his hands and a powerful tackler. Following Dick Huddart's move to St George in Sydney, Warlow went from strength to strength and he was selected for the Great Britain team against France in 1964. John was a member of the 1968 World Cup squad Down Under, together with his Saints' teammates Tommy Bishop and Cliff Watson. A Welsh international on three occasions, he captained his country in the 1969 international against France in Paris.

The Saints' pack laid the foundation for success in the mid-1960s and John began to pick up winner's medals on a regular basis. He played in the Saints' successful Western Division Championship team in 1964, together with a Lancashire Cup final success in 1964/65. The following season, he formed one of the biggest-ever back rows at Wembley, together with Ray French and John Mantle, in the 21-2 Challenge Cup victory over Wigan. In the semi-final, against Dewsbury at Swinton, his landlady, Minnie Cotton, came on to the pitch wielding her umbrella as retribution

for some rough play against her lodger – not that John couldn't look after himself, of course.

Although John was injured during the 1966 Championship final, he appeared in the 1967 final and replay, picking up Lancashire Cup winner's medals in 1967 and 1968. He moved to Widnes in 1970, captaining the Chemics to runner's up spots in the Lancashire Cup (1971) and Floodlit Trophy (1972). Then a masterstroke, as Saints brought him back to Knowsley Road in November 1973 and his experience helped the club to their one and only First Division Championship in 1974/75. Sadly, John was carried off injured in the Premiership final against Leeds at the end of the campaign, which St Helens lost; an unfortunate ending to a great career as a Saint.

John played for Rochdale Hornets for a short spell before retiring and moving back to South Wales. He will always be remembered as a player who was equally effective either in the front or second row, when the pack was used primarily to wear down the opposition for quality halves and three-quarters to finish the business. John is a member of the Saints' Past Players' Hall of Fame and a regular at the annual dinner at Knowsley Road.

Cliff Watson
Front-row forward 1960-1971

Previous club: Dudley Kingswinford RUFC

St Helens debut: 15 August 1960 v. Liverpool City

Final St Helens appearance: 7 May 1971 v. Leeds

Appearances: 367 + 6 subs

Tries: 57

Goals: 0

Points: 171

Transferred to: Cronulla Sutherland (Australia)

Representative honours: England, Great Britain

The search for big, powerful forwards knew no bounds during the summer of 1960, as the St Helens board took the unprecedented step of paying £400 for an advertising campaign in the national press, inviting top class rugby union packmen to write to Knowsley Road for trials. They received many replies, including this letter from Cliff Watson:

> In reply to your advertisement in the *Sporting Chronicle* for Rugby Football players, I offer you my services. I play rugby union football for Dudley Kingswinford as a second row forward and played open side prop for Worcestershire and Herefordshire combined counties last season. I am 20 years of age, 6ft tall and weigh 15st 6lbs. I should be grateful if you would consider my application.

Watson was invited for trials and duly signed for the club. It was a masterstroke. Cliff soon earned first team recognition and went on to become one of the most formidable players of the 1960s with thirty full appearances for Great Britain – the most capped prop forward in British rugby league.

Born in London's Mile End Road on 26 April 1940 – a true Cockney – Cliff was selected for his first big match after just ten games for the club, in the 1961 Challenge Cup final against Wigan at Wembley, where his superb cover tackle on Wigan's star winger Billy Boston ensured a Saints victory by 12-6. The early to mid-1960s saw the Saints crowned Cup Kings of Lancashire, with four consecutive successes, three times against Swinton (1961, 1962 and 1964) and once against Leigh (1963). Cliff played in them all and proved to be a durable member of a pack that contained other players imported from the union code, such as Ray French, John Warlow and John Mantle. Watson was naturally strong and his work as a drayman for Greenall Whitley certainly helped to keep him trim. He was a real grafter, who would take the ball up from his own line and was capable of crashing through opposing defences at the other end. Despite the loss of a finger on his left hand, his handling skills were not affected in the slightest. No-one liked being tackled by Cliff, in his all-embracing 'bear-hug' manner, and when the going got tough, he didn't take any prisoners – the perfect man to have by your side in the trenches.

In 1965/66 Watson and the St Helens pack were outstanding as the club won four trophies: League Leaders, Lancashire League, Championship and Challenge Cup – the latter against deadly rivals Wigan, in front of Wembley's first 100,000 crowd. Cliff won every major honour in the game with St Helens, playing in sixteen finals overall, including replays. He added to his collection of Lancashire Cup winner's medals with further successes in 1967 and 1969 and captained the side to one of their greatest triumphs – a 24-12 victory over a powerful Leeds' side at Odsal in 1970. This was his last final for the club, a broken arm robbing him of another Championship final appearance in 1971. He was immensely popular amongst the Knowsley Road faithful, who rewarded the 'Iron Man' with a successful testimonial cheque of over £3,000.

His physique and aggression were tailor-made for the rigours of Test match football, where he never took a backward step. He made his international debut at Swinton in the Second Test against Australia on 9 November 1963, a 50-12 victory for the Kangaroos; the first time the Ashes had been lost on home soil since 1911/12. Yet Watson became an automatic choice for his country, playing in an incredible eleven Tests against the Aussies until his last at the Sydney Cricket ground in 1970, when Britain won 21-17 to win the Ashes for the last time. He was selected for two tours Down Under in 1966 and 1970, also taking part in two World Cup campaigns, in 1968 and 1970. His clashes with Australians such as Arthur Beetson and Jim Morgan are not necessarily for the faint-hearted, but despite his 'hard man' image, he could also play superb football, typified by his twenty-yard blockbuster try in the First Test at the SCG in 1966.

Cliff was also great for team spirit. Former Saints' chairman Harry Cook recalled:

The fellow was a particular favourite of mine. One match day he came up to the directors' room with his boots, socks and shorts on – no jersey. I asked him what it was all about. 'They want to see you downstairs,' he said in a real gruff voice. 'And we're not putting our jerseys on until you come down.' So I thought – it must be money – because in those days they got so much per match, they didn't have contracts. So I went downstairs and asked them what the problem was. They all started laughing. 'We just wanted to see the look on your face when you came down!' said Cliff with a mischievous grin.

Watson joined the Australian club Cronulla at the start of the 1971/72 season, where his former Saints and Great Britain teammate Tommy Bishop was captain-coach. Cliff played in the 1973 Grand Final, when Cronulla lost to Manly and finished his career with a spell at the Wollongong junior club. He remains an Australian resident to this day.

Paul Wellens
Full-back 1999-

Previous club: Blackbrook ARLFC

St Helens debut: 30 August 1998 v. Halifax

Appearances: 201 + 25 subs

Tries: 86

Goals: 20

Points: 385

Transferred to:

Representative honours: Lancashire, England, Great Britain

Born in St Helens on 27 February 1980, Paul began his rugby career as a scrum-half at De La Salle School and later with Saints' Academy side. He was used in a utility role by coach Ellery Hanley during the 1999 campaign, which ended with Paul earning a place on the substitute's bench in the grand final against Bradford Bulls. Confident and mature beyond his years, it was obvious he was a star of the future.

His big break came in the first match of 2000 against Hull at the Boulevard, when the new Saints' coach, Ian Millward selected him at full-back in place of the injured Paul Atcheson. 'Wello' had a blinder that night, scored two excellent tries and earned the Man of the Match award. It was a real kick-start to his career and Paul has never looked back. At the end of the season, twenty-year-old Wellens found himself playing a more major role in Saints' back-to-back Grand Final success against Wigan at Old Trafford, with selection for the England World Cup squad just reward for his achievements. Although England were well beaten by New Zealand in the semi-finals, it was clear that Paul had a promising international career ahead of him.

A brainy footballer, with great technique in both attack and defence, Paul was a member of the Saints' team that lifted the World Club Championship by defeating Brisbane Broncos at Bolton in 2001, during which he suffered a fractured eye socket. At

international level, he made his full Great Britain debut against France and played twice against the Australians in the Ashes series. A Challenge Cup victory against Bradford Bulls at Twickenham brought Paul his first winner's medal in 2001, although 2002 brought somewhat contrasting fortunes, with Saints losing in the Challenge Cup final against Wigan at Murrayfield and Paul receiving an horrific cheekbone injury early in the Grand Final, when Bradford Bulls were the opposition once again. He was putting his body on the line by clearing up a grubber kick when the injury happened, which subsequently required the insertion of plates into his cheekbone.

A fantastic competitor, Paul had an was quite superb in Saints' 32-16 defeat of rivals Wigan in the 2004 Challenge Cup final at Cardiff, scoring a crucial try under the posts just before half-time with his typical strength and guile. Once again, he was outstanding at international level in the Tri-Nations competition, reaching the final with Great Britain after the side topped the table. Although the Australians won the final comprehensively, Paul could stand favourable comparison with the world's great full-backs Anthony Minichello of Australia and New Zealand's Brent Webb. Given the measure of his achievements so far and what he is capable of in the future, Paul will undoubtedly become an all-time great at Knowsley Road – an immensely likable lad who loves rugby league and is a perfect role model for youngsters.

Previous club: Kendal Hornets

St Helens debut: 7 September 1893 v. Rochdale Hornets

Final St Helens appearance: 25 December 1907 v. Runcorn

Appearances: 311

Tries: 23

Goals: 0

Points: 69

Transferred to: Retired

Representative honours: None

There have been many great forward signings from what is now called Cumbria, with the likes of Dick Huddart, John Tembey and Jon Neill springing to mind. One of the best was William Whiteley, a lad from Staveley, Kendal, who came south in 1893 and ended up having a forty-seven-year connection with the St Helens club, as player, turnstile checker and groundsman.

Bill first played as a full-back for Kendal Town RFC at the age of seventeen, before moving to the famous Kendal Hornets club, where he became a county representative. In June 1893, he followed his old club-mate Billy Cross to St Helens and quickly established a reputation as one of the hardest and fastest forwards in the north of England. Whiteley was a key member of the side that won the Lancashire County Second Division title in 1894 and played on the wing in the first-ever rugby league match at Knowsley Road against Rochdale two years later. As a twenty-five-year-old, Bill was in the second row for the first-ever Challenge Cup final, played at Headingley against the eventual winners Batley in 1897.

The early years of the twentieth century were not easy for the Saints, as they endured a 'yo-yo' existence between the First and Second Divisions. Yet Bill Whiteley would always give nothing less than 100 per cent commitment to the cause. He was a member of the team that won the South West Lancashire and Border Towns Cup final, against Leigh, at Widnes, in 1900. Yet in truth, the team rarely challenged for major honours, although Bill helped the team to promotion back into the First Division at the end of the 1903/04 campaign and played against the visiting New Zealand and Australian touring teams.

On Saturday, 7 May 1910, a benefit match was staged for Bill at his beloved Knowsley Road, with the Saints taking on the might of Turtill's Colonials, a side assembled from New Zealanders in England, including famous names such as George Smith, Charlie Seeling and Lance Todd. Captained by Saints' full-back 'Jum' Turtill, the visitors won a spectacular match by 40-24 and travelled to St Helens at their own expense to pay tribute to a marvellous rugby stalwart. The game took place despite the death of the reigning monarch, Edward VII earlier in the day.

During Bill's time, the players stripped at the Talbot Hotel in Duke Street. They then boarded a horse-drawn wagonette for the journey to Knowsley Road and Bill would often run back to the dressing rooms instead of returning on the wagon. By 1940, he had to resign as groundsman because of bad arthritis in his legs – undoubtedly caused by lingering too long in cold, wet playing togs. Bill was devoted to the club and was made a life member, together with his former teammates Tom Foulkes and Bill Briers. No-one deserved it more than him.

Frank Wilson
Winger 1968-1976

Previous club: Cardiff RUFC

St Helens debut: 20 August 1968 v. Whitehaven

Final St Helens appearance: 16 May 1976 v. Leeds

Appearances: 301 + 9 subs

Tries: 176

Goals: 0

Points: 528

Transferred to: Workington Town

Representative honours: Wales

When he first signed for the Saints from Cardiff RUFC in 1968, Frank Wilson had the near-impossible task of replacing the legendary Tom van Vollenhoven. It is a fitting testimony to his football ability that he became a true St Helens great, making over 300 appearances for the club, scoring 176 tries. Born in Cardiff, Frank had progressed through the union ranks, playing in a final Welsh trial, before the Saints signed him on 20 August 1968, despite interest from rivals Wigan. He adapted brilliantly to his new code and soon began to demonstrate his wide range of skills, including lightning speed off the mark, a mesmerising body swerve and the ability to maintain his pace over long distances. He was also a terrific defender, who could blot out an opponent, if required to do so. Frank won his first honour as a Saint in the 1968 Lancashire Cup final against Oldham, when he scored two brilliant tries in his team's 30-2 success.

He finished his first campaign with twenty-five touchdowns and looked forward to further glory with the club. Yet he was to miss two consecutive Championship finals over the next few years. Somewhat unorthodox in his approach, he sometimes made errors of judgement. One such gaffe in the Championship semi-final against Castleford (despite scoring a superb hat-trick) influenced

coach Cliff Evans to leave him out of the 1970 clash with Leeds at Odsal. He was replaced by second-rower Eric Prescott, who potentially spared the coach's blushes with a fine display. In 1971, after another fine season, Frank missed the final against Wigan after picking up an injury and was replaced by Bob Blackwood.

Wilson made 40 appearances during the 1971/72 campaign, scoring 17 tries and was an integral member of the side that lifted the BBC2 Floodlit Trophy and the Challenge Cup final against Leeds at Wembley. He did a superb defensive job on his opposite number, Alan Smith, and made several vital runs into enemy territory as pressure mounted on his teammates. Frank picked up a First Division Championship medal in 1974/75, operating mostly as centre to Les Jones. A further BBC2 success against Dewsbury followed in 1975/76 and just when the business end of the season approached, he missed out on a second Wembley appearance as a result of a niggling injury, with coach Eric Ashton handing over one substitute spot to Peter Glynn before the final against Widnes.

Frank moved on to Workington at the end of the campaign and played with distinction for Salford, before a final season with the Cardiff Blue Dragons in 1981/82, together with his former Saints' teammates Tony Karalius and George Nicholls. He also represented his native Wales with distinction on fourteen occasions, making his debut against England at Salford in 1968 on the right wing and took part in the 1975 World Championships in Australia and New Zealand.

Other titles published by Stadia

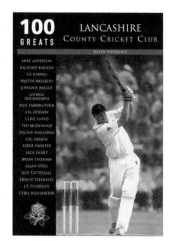

Lancashire CCC 100 Greats
KEITH HAYHURST

This book celebrates 100 of the best players to have represented Lancashire CCC since the club was formed in 1864. From the exceptional amateurs that dominated the team in the early years, through the heroes of the late 1960s that made Lancashire the kings of one-day cricket, to modern heroes such as Michael Atherton and Andrew Flintoff, this publication includes biographies, statistics and illustrations of Lancashire's finest.

0 7524 2405 X

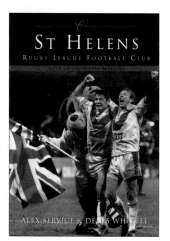

St Helens RLFC Classic Matches
ALEX SERVICE & DENIS WHITTLE

This book contains a selection of matches recognised as classic encounters for a variety of reasons. It provides a fascinating journey through the history of rugby league – beginning with the first Challenge Cup final in 1897 and ending with the Saints being crowned World Champions after beating the Brisbane Broncos in 2001. This well-illustrated volume is a real treasure trove of memories and is a must for Saints and rugby league fans alike.

0 7524 2706 7

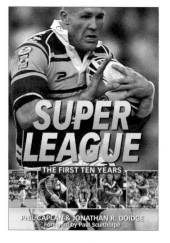

Super League The First Ten Years
PHIL CAPLAN & JONATHAN R. DOIDGE

In March 1996, 100 years after its formation, rugby league undertook the biggest re-branding exercise seen in modern sport with a switch to summer and the formation of a twelve-team Super League. In an extensive, unique analysis, the roots behind this radical conversion are explored, looking at the historical context and the business imperatives that govern top-level sport in the modern era.

0 7524 3698 8

If you are interested in purchasing other books published by Stadia, or in case you have difficulty finding any Stadia books in your local bookshop, you can also place orders directly through the Tempus Publishing website

www.tempus-publishing.com